Φικεία

THE MANUAL OF PHI DELTA THETA

Printed in the United States of America by Maury Boyd & Associates of Indianapolis, Indiana.

Thirty-seventh Edition.

BOOK DESIGN BY DAVID C. SLATTON

Φικεία

The Manual

of
Phi Delta Theta

Thirty-Seventh Edition
2004-2006

EDITED BY
The Phi Delta Theta General Headquarters Staff

Table of Contents

The Phikeia Oath

I now declare that I pledge myself and my services to the Phi Delta Theta Fraternity. That I will discharge faithfully the duties devolving upon me as a Phikeia, and that I will try to promote the welfare of the Fraternity, and that I will be always mindful of the basic principles of the Fraternity. And further, I pledge myself as a college man to uphold the honor and dignity of Phi Delta Theta, everywhere and at all times. I will never bring disgrace to this, my Fraternity, by any act of dishonesty or moral cowardice. I will stand firm for the ideals and sacred things of my Fraternity, both alone and with my Phikeia brothers. I will revere and obey the laws of the Fraternity, and do my best to incite a like respect and reverence in my Phikeia brothers and in every member of this chapter. I will strive in all ways to transmit the Fraternity to those who may follow after, not only not less, but greater than it was transmitted to me.

Preface to the 37th Edition

THE FIRST MANUAL OF Phi Delta Theta was printed in 1886 under the authorship of Walter B. Palmer, *Emory-Vanderbilt 1877*. In the preface to that first publication Brother Palmer gives credit to J. Marshall Mayer, *C.C.N.Y. 1884*, managing editor of THE SCROLL, for proposing the idea that a manual be printed. The small 4½"x 6" booklet contained 54 pages and was devoted primarily to an early history of the Fraternity. It included a short list of prominent members, a few facts on other fraternities, and vital statistics on the colleges and universities where chapters of Phi Delta Theta had been established.

The second edition of the Manual edited by Palmer followed the same general outline of the first except that the history was recorded to date, the words to a few songs were added, and pictures of four chapter houses were displayed. This edition was issued as a supplement to THE SCROLL in October of 1897 and was sent to all subscribers.

The third edition was prepared by Palmer and printed in 1912. It was somewhat of a summary of his history published in 1906. The Manual was renamed THE OLYMPIAN OF PHI DELTA THETA and contained 316 pages. Although the general outline of the material was the same, there were numerous pictures of chapter houses and Phi dignitaries. Many cuts from the history were utilized in this manual.

The fourth and fifth editions edited by Executive Secretary Arthur R. Priest, *DePauw 1891*, reverted to the approximate size of the original manual. Brother Priest prepared much of the material which has been retained in the manual as it appears today. He introduced a chapter on "How to Study" which was deleted when his work was revised. The Priest book was entitled THE PHIKEIA, HIS BOOK.

The sixth edition was prepared by Edward E. Ruby, *Indiana 1897*, editor of THE SCROLL. This edition took on the size of our current manual and followed closely the pattern established by Priest. Ruby's Manual of Phi Delta Theta was printed in 1938.

Executive Secretary Paul C. Beam, *Indiana-Illinois '25*, revised Ruby's work in 1942. When the seventh edition was printed, the word Φικεια was added to the title. Aside from the addition of one or two chapters and the deletion of less important material, this edition was essentially the same as the sixth. The eighth through fourteenth editions were all prepared by Brother Beam and were printed approximately every two years.

The fifteenth edition of the Manual, edited by Executive Vice President Robert J. Miller, *New Mexico '50,* was a reproduction of its predecessor, bringing up to date all the statistics contained therein. The next seven editions followed the same pattern, with the only significant change being the deletion of the complete collection of chapter house pictures which, in the past, consumed 40 pages. A change of style and format highlighted the twenty-third to twenty-fifth editions, as was immediately evident in a new size, 7" x 7¼".

Several significant changes were made in the twenty-sixth edition. Major changes were made in four chapters and a new chapter was added for the sake of clarity.

Brother Miller prepared the fifteenth through the twenty-ninth editions approximately once every two years.

Minor statistical changes were made to the thirtieth edition by Executive Vice President, Robert A. Biggs, *Georgia Southern '76.*

Major changes were made in the format and content of the thirty-first edition. A hardbound cover was used, and the format was altered to 7"x 9". Many chapters were rewritten, while some chapters from the original version remained. Chapters on scholarship and risk management were added, and a complete copy of *The Code* of Phi Delta Theta was appended to The Manual.

The content of this, the thirty-seventh edition, has been altered to meet the needs of Phi Delta Theta's active chapters. The section on Risk Management has been expanded to address many of the issues encountered by the fraternity in greater clarity and detail, and to address the alcohol-free housing initiative being implemented this year. Many photos have been updated in The Manual to illustrate the ideals and principles outlined within the content. Other updates were made to reflect changes in Phi Delta Theta over the past two years and make this manual accurate in every detail.

ROBERT A. BIGGS, GEORGIA SOUTHERN '76
Executive Vice President
August, 2004

The FEA Statement of Position on Hazing and Pre-Initiation Activities

The Association believes that true fraternalism is nurtured in an atmosphere of social and moral responsibility, respect for duly constituted authority and loyalty to the principles of higher education.

"The Association further believes that while social behavior cannot be legislated, a fraternity without morally sound precepts and practices is not a constructive influence upon college students.

"The Association further believes that a fraternity has a solemn obligation in the development of its pledges/associate members and that this responsibility extends alike to the institutions where it is represented; to parents and others who make possible the education of pledges/associates and members; to the communities where chapters are accountable for good citizenship; and to the college fraternity system of which it is a part.

"The Association further believes that while much progress has been made, one of the most damaging instruments to the fraternity system is the employment of a program of education which includes hazing, and that this unproductive, ridiculous and hazardous custom has no rightful place in the fraternity system.

"The Association defines hazing as any action taken or situation created, intentionally, whether on or off fraternity premises, to produce mental or physical discomfort, embarrassment, harassment or ridicule. Such activities and situations include paddling in any form; creation of excessive fatigue; physical and psychological shocks; quests, treasure hunts, scavenger hunts, road trips or any other such activities carried on outside the confines of the house; wearing, publicly, apparel which is conspicuous and not normally in good taste; engaging in public stunts and buffoonery; morally degrading or humiliating games and activities; late work sessions which interfere with scholastic activities; and any other activities which are not consistent with fraternal law, ritual or policy or the regulations and policies of the educational institution.

The Fraternity Executives Association is an organization made up of executives from many of the national and international fraternities and sororities. It has supported positive educational pledge programming and condemned hazing and other unconstructive pre-initiation activities as antithetical to the mission of fraternal organizations. As a Fraternity interested in the well-being and education of its members and Phikeias, Phi Delta Theta supports the above position.

I

The Phikeia Program

FEW EXPERIENCES IN a man's time in this world are more important to him than those shared with his closest friends. Whether it is the drudgery of daily routine or seeing new and exciting places for the first time, having comrades with him makes these times special now and will preserve memories for the distant future.

This is the essence of fraternity life. Brotherhood is a word that defies definition to those who have not had firsthand experience in Greek life. The mention of it may bring stereotypical images of guys playing football and talking about cars or parties, but brotherhood is much more than that. Brotherhood is a feeling that comes from the experiences shared with close friends. It transcends typical friendship, becoming a familial relationship.

Definitions of brotherhood are very personal and very different. True brotherhood may be the closest tie you have with your fellow men. It is a sense of belonging, but it is also an understanding of a man's worthiness to be part of a special group which has achieved great things. It is a family, the closest equivalent to a home away from home.

The friendships you make while in college will perhaps be the most important relationships you develop in your life. Seeing alumni return to your campus year after year, sharing stories of their old college days reminds us that life in Phi Delta Theta is no mere campus interlude, it is brotherhood for a lifetime.

Phi Delta Theta is often called the "Fraternity for Life," because of its lifelong commitment to the values and experiences of its members. A new Phikeia embarks on this lifelong journey to discover his own definition of brotherhood by sharing college experiences with fellow Phikeias and the members of the Fraternity. The Phikeia will learn valuable

---

Facing Page: Founders John Wolfe Lindley (standing) and Robert Morrison at the semi-centennial Convention in Columbus, Ohio, 1898.

lessons of life, the lessons that cannot be taught in the classroom. He will learn how to manage an organization, to lead and to follow, to develop himself as a person. Most importantly, he will understand the imperfections in himself and in others and learn to overcome those shortcomings. He will share some of the greatest moments of triumph and accomplishment with the men he will call brothers.

The Phikeia Program

Fraternity life has a development period, commonly referred to as pledgeship. In Phi Delta Theta, this time is known as the Phikeia Program. This period is designed to prepare men to take on the obligations of full membership. As a Phikeia, a man is instructed in the history, life, principles, and lore of the Fraternity so that he may have an appreciation of the organization he is joining.

In Phi Delta Theta a young man who has been invited to become a member, and who has accepted this invitation by his formal pledge, may wear a pin and is known as a *Phikeia.*

Every Phikeia takes a formal oath, which he signs in the presence of witnesses.

In making this pledge and becoming a Phikeia, a man surrenders none of his legal or social rights, none of his family or personal ties, none of his moral or religious ideals and standards. His status as a free individual changes only in that he has voluntarily taken on a new responsibility which gives him a unique opportunity to develop himself by following the ideals of Phi Delta Theta.

In becoming a Phikeia, the young college man becomes his brother's keeper. He is interested in every man in the chapter, and every member and Phikeia is interested in him. The Phikeia, just as the member, is expected to conduct his personal life—both on and off campus—in a manner which will al-

BUILDING BROTHERHOOD.
Teamwork and having fun are two important aspects of fraternity life.

ways reflect creditably on Phi Delta Theta and on himself.

As a Phikeia, a man begins to live the ideals of Phi Delta Theta on a daily basis. These are ideals which he will promise to make his own in a very solemn way when he becomes a member. During this developmental period, he begins to work to maintain high standards of scholarship, to make his contribution to campus life through various activities, and to build friendships with those with whom he is associated.

Living as a Phikeia, one learns to share the financial burden of the chapter. Here one learns to pay financial obligations promptly and to budget funds well. The chapter treasurer must pay bills promptly and for this reason each Phikeia and member must pay his share and not force others to pay his way for him.

Prior to becoming a member of the chapter and holding full membership as a Phi, the Phikeia participates in an educational program. In this way, he develops an appreciation of the Fraternity and of the men who have gone before him as members. During this period, he will participate in a variety of activities with his Phikeia brothers and with the entire chapter, including community service, alumni events, fund-raising and social functions. These activities are designed to educate the Phikeia about the operations of the chapter as well as instill a bond of brotherhood with his fellow Phikeias and the chapter members.

Participating in these activities as a Phikeia, the man learns what duties must be performed and what obligations are expected of him throughout membership in Phi Delta Theta. He learns how to do his part to contribute to having a smooth-running chapter. These tasks are not to interfere with regular college work, but they require each Phikeia to plan ahead and accept responsibility. It is in completing these tasks that a young man learns to serve so that later he may lead.

The educational time before becoming a voting member is a time of adjustment to fraternity living and to college life. The Phikeia fiinds himself away from family and high school friends. No one is there telling him when to study or how to do it. There are new friendships to form, more demands to produce scholastically, new ways to live.

Part of this formation period for the Phikeia may bring advice and development from the fraternity members. Given in a spirit of helpfulness, this will aid in the growth and development for life after college. At times every individual may think that he has the answers to life's questions Yet every type of assistance comes with the desire to improve personally and as a chapter. It is the mature man who benefits by whatever constructive criticism comes his way.

The period of pledgeship is not a one-way street, however. The members of the Fraternity have obligations as well. The chapter is responsible for providing a constructive program of Phikeia education and mentorship. Upperclassmen must set the example and model as well as standards for the Phikeia. General Headquarters provides a manual to help the chapter in this program of Phikeia development and education. Hazing is strictly forbidden. There is no place in Phi Delta Theta for activities which are harmful, vulgar, or degrading. The traditions of Phi Delta Theta have always stressed building men up, not tearing them down.

The College

As one begins college life during the orientation process, new introductions come one's way: the institution's history, faculty members, and landmarks become important as a foundation for the years to be experienced on the campus. The new student is led by a competent guide. Here the "spirit" of the school is described with the hope that the new man will "catch" that spirit and become a loyal member of the student body.

Phi Delta Theta has always insisted on loyalty to one's college or university. Loyalty to one's academic institution can easily be applied to one's fraternity. Phi Delta Theta recognizes that the college or university makes possible the Fraternity, and for this reason, every member of the fraternity owes to his college or university his loyalty and unswerving support. If any Phikeia sets out to be a wisely loyal college man, he will find himself becoming a worthily loyal Fraternity man. In turn, by being a good fraternity man, he becomes closely tied to his college or university and upon graduation sees his loyalty bound by two strong ties which mutually strengthen each other.

Courtesy

The chapter house or lodge is the Fraternity home of the Phikeia and the chapter. He will be expected to show courtesy to guests and share responsibility for the facility. To always be polite and gentlemanly, whatever the tasks laid on them, a Phikeia should bear in mind always that he is a member of the organization and responsible for the reputation of the chapter and its hospitality.

Each Phikeia discovers that with the privileges of membership comes certain responsibilities, and that he must be a contributing representative of the Fraternity. He discovers that no fraternity chapter remains successful by resting on the laurels of past accomplishments. The sooner he prepares himself for the active role he must fulfill as an initiated member, the sooner he finds the true meaning of brotherhood.

Not until the Phikeia becomes a member, looking back on himself as a Phikeia through the eyes of new men who are being recruited and pledged, does he understand fully the importance of the educational period which precedes initiation.

The house or lodge of the chapter should be attractive enough to hold the interest of every member. Members should keep it clean and well organized. The chapter should also offer an outlet for unselfish service. Chapter life cannot measure up to these standards unless every Phikeia has responded to the sure tests of character, education, and ability of the Phikeia Program.

Big Brothers

Near the beginning of the program, the Phikeia Educator will start the process of assigning or matching each Phikeia to a Big Brother. A Big Brother is an initiated member of the Fraternity who becomes the Phikeia's mentor. He helps the Phikeia to adjust to college life, to acquaint himself with the chapter, and to complete the Phikeia program. Big Brothers serve as role models and teachers.

Often the chapter will schedule events just for the Big Brothers and "little brothers" to help them develop a special bond that is so important in the Fraternity. There will be many times during the first year of college life when the trials of school or the adjustments of everyday life will make things difficult for a Phikeia. A Big Brother can be a great help during these times.

Phikeia Officers & Meetings

Organization of the Phikeia class takes place shortly after the formal induction ceremony. The president of the chapter or the Phikeia Educator will assemble the new men for organization just as soon as all are thoroughly acquainted.

Officers will explain the status of a Phikeia, and will outline expectations of Phikeia activities. A committee of new Phikeias may be appointed to also formulate expectations for the entire class. This group may set forth duties, name committees and plan for organization of the class. Phikeia class officers will then be chosen—a president, secretary, and treasurer at a minimum. These officers will preside over all meetings of the class, although the Phikeia Educator will be present at all sessions, serving in a supervisory capacity and as liaison officer between the Phikeia class and the chapter.

Phikeia meetings will be conducted according to the accepted rules of parliamentary procedure. Generally, business will include the following:

- Roll Call
- Minutes of Last Meeting
- Reports of Officers
- Reports of Committees
- Scholarship Reports
- Old Business
- New Business
- Announcements
- Examination on Assigned Material
- Guest Speaker
- Assignments

This is the same type of general organization used by the chapter, and it should be used by the class to better prepare the Phikeias to take on the full responsibility of membership when they are initiated.

During the Phikeia period it is beneficial to remember that Phikeia do have a voice within the chapter and are expected to play a vital role in the chapter. Always remember that there are opportunities to make suggestions through the Big Brother, the Phikeia Educator, and the chapter advisory board. One of the most effective means is through the formal weekly Phikeia meeting.

Always bear in mind that the Phikeia program is a period of learning. The Phikeia will not be subjected to harsh treatment nor to indignities. As a Phikeia he should remember that there are tasks to perform, but hazing is strictly forbidden by the Fraternity. If he performs well during the Phikeia period, the Phikeia will be a better man, and he will be much happier and better educated. Phi Delta Theta is interested in making the individual a better man than he would have been had he not joined the Fraternity.

Social Etiquette

An outstanding characteristic of fraternity men everywhere is their social poise and skill in meeting and communicating with people. One of the marks of an educated man is good manners. One of the best places to acquire this mark is in a well-conducted fraternity chapter. The Phikeia should gain an understanding of the basic fundamentals of social

The Greek Alphabet

A, α .. Alpha	H, η ... Eta	N. ν ... Nu	T, τ .... Tau
B, β ... Beta	Θ, θ ... Theta	Ξ, ξ ... Xi	Y, υ ... Upsilon
Γ, γ .... Gamma	I, ι ..... Iota	O, o ... Omicron	Φ, φ ... Phi
Δ, δ ... Delta	K, κ ... Kappa	Π, π ... Pi	X, χ ... Chi
E, ε .... Epsilon	Λ, λ ... Lambda	P, ρ ... Rho	Ψ, ψ .. Psi
Z, ζ ... Zeta	M, μ .. Mu	Σ, σ ... Sigma	Ω, ω .. Omega

etiquette. What follows is a general guide for the situations a Phikeia may encounter from day-to-day.

Introductions should be formal when presenting one person to another, yet introductions need not be confusing. The name of the person whom you are introducing is mentioned first, for example, "Mr. Guest, may I present Mr. Member." A woman's name is generally mentioned first. Introduce a gentleman to a lady, a member to a guest, and a young person to a markedly older person. When introducing two women, the younger is presented to the older. In introducing either a young man or a young woman to an older, distinguished man or woman, the distinguished person's name is given the preferred position, as "General Patton, this is Mr. Roberts," or "Dr. Taylor, let me present Miss Patterson." Gentlemen always shake hands. Men always rise when introductions are being made. An accepted reply to an introduction is simply, "How do you do?" Repeating the name once may help you remember it. Introductions are very important in social relations, for they provide first impressions which may never be entirely forgotten.

Dining room conduct is yet another area where the Phikeia can demonstrate his social poise. Naturally, guests and ladies should enter the dining room first. Everyone should remain standing until grace has been said. Permit female guests to take their seats first, then gentlemen are to be seated.

The general rule of thumb when using silverware is to work from the outside in. That is, the utensils used for the first course such as a salad fork or a soup spoon are placed furthest from the plate; continue toward the plate as the courses progress. Of course, when in doubt, follow the lead of your host. When drinking any beverage at the table a sip is never taken until the mouth is empty and has been wiped with a napkin. This keeps the rim of your cup or glass free from food marks. Napkins can be properly placed on the lap, entirely open if they are lunch-size, or in half if they are dinner napkins. The men should wait until female guests have taken up their napkins before placing theirs in their laps. Napkins may only be tucked in if riding on an airplane. At the conclusion of the meal, napkins are gathered and laid casually to the left of the place setting—they are never refolded. The tipping of a soup or dessert dish is acceptable provided the dish is tipped away from the eater and not toward him. The utensil then is likewise tipped away from the body to gather the desired portion. There is absolutely no excuse for vulgar language at the dinner table. Topics of conversation should be of the less controversial nature. Save the political debate for the after dinner hours. Avoid squeamish subjects (accidents, operations, etc.), and do not raise your voice above a conversational tone. If you must leave the table for any reason, no explanation is necessary, simply nod to the host or hostess and make the request, "May I be excused?" When returning to the table, take your place without comment. Again, at the end of the meal, place your napkin to the left of your table setting and rise as the host rises.

Telephone etiquette includes promptness, eagerness to be of service, and courtesy in responding to the call is an indication of the Phikeia's interest in the chapter's welfare and his consideration for others. The chapter's telephone should be answered, "Phi Delta Theta, how may I help you?" Answering the telephone in a long, drawn-out manner is unnecessary and a nuisance. Calmly notify the person called that he is wanted on the telephone or take a message. When there is someone at the door, ask the visitor kindly what the nature of his business is. If the visitor is a guest, escort him in and introduce him to others present.

An individual's dress is often times the basis for a stranger's first impression. Though individuality should exist, proper attire for a wide variety of settings is a must. A gentleman knows the rules of dress and abides by them.

In conclusion, it should be pointed out that this brief synopsis on the laws of manners and conduct is by no means an all-inclusive one. A Phikeia should observe these few fundamentals of social etiquette while also learning from the members of the chapter.

Conventional Greek Vocabulary

Upon entering the Greek world, a Phikeia must become familiar with its conventions to be used in dealings with alumni and interfraternal friends.

The correct term for a male graduate is *alumnus.* "Alum" or any other abbreviation is not appropriate. The plural is *alumni.* These terms apply to the chapter's alumni as well as to other Greek and non-Greek alumni from the institution. The correct term for a female graduate is *alumna.* The plural is *alumnae* (pronounced, alum-nee).

Never refer to the fraternity as a "frat." It is an improper colloquialism and its use shows the speaker as unversed in fraternity lore. Members refer to Phi Delta Theta as a *fraternity* and extend the same courtesy to other Greeks as well.

Phikeias and members should use "brothers" when referring to initiated members of Phi Delta Theta. Refrain from the archaic "brethren."

Some people may often use the term "house" when they really mean "chapter." Some chapters do not have houses, but even those that do are still chapters. A chapter is made up of the men who are members of it. A house is merely a structure.

Another common error is a reference to the General Fraternity or General Headquarters as "Nationals." This is incorrect usage and has been since 1902 when Phi Delta Theta installed its first Canadian chapter at McGill University in Quebec. Phi Delta Theta should be referenced as the General or International Headquarters.

Questions

1. What is a Phikeia?
2. What is the purpose of the Phikeia education program?
4. Who are your Phikeia class officers, and what is each one's job?
5. What is a Big Brother?
6. What is the order of procedure for a Phikeia meeting?
7. What is a male graduate called? The plural? A female graduate? The plural?
8. What is wrong with the using the word "Nationals?"
9. Write and spell the letters of the Greek alphabet.

Essays

1. Give a personal definition of brotherhood.
2. Why is social etiquette important? Is it practiced properly at your chapter?

II

*"Phi Delta Theta was organized with three principle
objectives: The cultivation of friendship among its
members; the acquirement individually of a high degree
of mental culture, and the attainment personally of a
high standard of morality."*
WALTER B. PALMER, EMORY-VANDERBILT 1877

Three Cardinal Principles

THE OBJECTIVES OR principles of Phi Delta Theta were never more clearly and simply set forth than in an analysis written by Walter B. Palmer, *Emory-Vanderbilt 1877,* to George Banta Sr., *Franklin-Indiana 1876.* These two men, frequently referred to as the "Second Founders," probably contributed more to the building of Phi Delta Theta as an international brotherhood than have any other men.

Palmer wrote: "Phi Delta Theta was organized with three principle objectives: the cultivation of friendship among its members; the acquirement individually of a high degree of mental culture, and the attainment personally of a high standard of morality. These objectives are declared in The Bond of Phi Delta Theta, which every member admitted to the Fraternity pledges himself to uphold. The same pledge has been taken by every member since the organization of the Fraternity in 1848, and so long as Phi Delta Theta shall exist, The Bond will remain inviolate and unalterable.

"Primarily the Fraternity is a social organization. It is the duty of members to render mutual assistance to one another in all honorable undertakings. The intimate intercourse between members results in much social enjoyment during college life and many enduring friendships in after years. Secrecy concerning the organization is perpetually and wisely enjoyed in The Bond, not because secrecy is a vital factor, but it is important where friendships are so close and confidential. The Fraternity seeks to throw around its members the influences of the home. A proper degree of privacy concerning itself is an essential to the Order. The privacy of the family circle renders possible the development of character which could not be attained without it, and for the same end Phi Delta Theta carries the element of privacy into the associations of the young men who have come from their homes and united with this college brotherhood.

Facing Page: Walter B. Palmer, his wife and daughter at the General Convention in 1902. Palmer is the author of the principles as we understand them today.

"The spirit of the Fraternity is well embodied in the mutual pledge, 'All for one and one for all.'"

The three principle objectives, also referred to as the three cardinal principles, described by Walter B. Palmer, are briefly stated as "friendship, sound learning, and rectitude."

Friendship

Fraternal living is often described as providing an experience in group interaction. While this is one of the elements found whenever people are together, Phi Delta Theta sees much more in its principle of friendship.

Every group will have some give-and-take. This experience can be on a very low superficial level or it can be on a highly intense level. The Phikeia who wishes to become a member of Phi Delta Theta will need to take time to examine the demands of friendship. True friendship gives more and takes less. True friendship, for one who strives to act maturely, will raise the question, "What can I give?" rather than, "What is in it for me?"

College fraternities are frequently referred to as "Greek letter societies." The Greek letters which give most fraternities their names are more than just letters. Most fraternities and sororities—at least from the view of their founders—saw in the Ancient Greeks and Romans ideals which they felt should be restated and lived.

The friendship enjoyed by Socrates at Athens has been a model for centuries, for people have seen in that band of Greek men something worthy of imitation, interest and appeal. There was a physical and cultural

ADOPT-A-SCHOOL PROGRAM.
Fulfilling the principle of Rectitude often means participating in service programs like the National Interfraternity Conference's Adopt-A-School program where collegians help underprivileged children.

heritage which served as a basis for friendship. Friendship was more than simple camaraderie! It was this ideal that served as a basis for the formation of Phi Delta Theta by its founders. Robert Morrison, an exceptional scholar in Greek and Latin, knew the ideals expressed by the classical authors and one of these ideals was that of friendship.

The classical Greek and Roman writers—Socrates and others—saw friendship as a unity of skills, tastes and thoughts. This was not a loss of personal identity, but rather a search for truth and a desire to be united with others who sought the same. In this search, men would make an adjustment to each other—an adjustment which would come from mutual goodwill and affection.

The good man is one who is of strong character, just and generous in his friendship, loyal and upright. Friendship is born between men who share these ideals.

The classical authors mention the duties of friendship: truthfulness, mutual correction, fidelity. Friendship's law will never ask another to do wrong or encourage him in wrongdoing.

We see in this classical model that friendship is more than simply being together. True friendship demands a great deal. One must be ready to make sacrifices for the demands of friendship.

It is here that the Phikeia is challenged! Can he live a life of friendship with his Phikeia brothers? Is he willing to develop this friendship with every member of his chapter? There is much give-and-take in group life and the Phikeia along with the members must raise his sights and be genial and kind. Is the Phikeia ready to stand against those who would propose actions which are not in conformity with right ideals and living?

Many chapters of Phi Delta Theta have a program of Big Brothers to help the Phikeia along the way of development. Here the Phikeia has a unique chance to develop and try out the elements of friendship. The challenge, of course, comes during this period of pledgeship in that the Phikeia must learn to discriminate and pick his models from among the men of sterling worth—and not from chance campus heroes.

The principle of friendship in Phi Delta Theta, as viewed by the "Immortal Six Founders," challenges the members of the Fraternity to a mutual affection which builds up the other, helps to strengthen him as he moves and works through life. Friendship brings forth a mutual confidence in the friend-to-friend relationship.

As a man grows in the collegiate environment, he comes to see that this ideal of friendship is one that will serve him well throughout life.

Sound Learning

The ideal of scholarship is very important in the life of the Fraternity, and it was an ideal very evident in the lives of the Founders. The most important thing about good scholarship is that it comes about only if one has the will to study and the desire to penetrate beyond the surface—if the student is willing to do more than just get by with the "gentleman's C" grade.

The primary reason for attending college is to study and to learn. Scholarship achievement and fraternal living must complement each other.

Sound learning does not immediately imply scholarship, but intellectual curiosity and a search for truth. However, high scholastic achievement is almost impossible without a sense of intellectual curiosity and a drive for truth and understanding. The good student is one who is excited about learning and is driven to knowledge. Once that curiosity is combined with a sound work ethic, academic achievement is a relatively simple matter.

Many chapters have scholarship programs with study halls, quiet hours, group study sessions, scholarship awards, and time management seminars. These programs are designed to maximize members' efforts in class. The programs also emphasize the importance of scholarship to the chapter and help ensure that the chapter is a positive influence within the campus community.

Chapter VII of this manual discusses some strategies to use in studying. Time management, reading and lecture techniques, and test-taking skills play an important role in preparing for classes. A good student must remember, however, that nothing can replace an honest desire to learn.

Rectitude

As an historical fact, it is important to remember that the "Immortal Six" were strongly Christian men. Robert Morrison was a preacher for 14 years; Wilson became a pastor; Drake was ordained in Iowa and served in three states; Rodgers was ordained as a Presbyterian minister. The moral strength of these men led them to see one of the principles of the fraternity they founded to be a commitment to a moral standard.

It is probably unfortunate that the word "rectitude" frequently brings on simplistic thoughts of going to church or abstaining from alcohol. WEBSTER'S NINTH NEW COLLEGIATE DICTIONARY includes in its definition of rectitude the idea of moral integrity or correctness of judgment.

Rectitude has more to do with the way a man approaches living and less with observing dos and don'ts. Some people think of the moral code of the Ten Commandments when it comes to moral integrity, but a proper understanding of the nature of rectitude goes far beyond rule-keeping.

OHIO WESLEYAN PHIS, 1884.

In college, the Phikeia may find himself in a difficult period of transition. He begins to live outside a family structure and has to deal with a variety of personalities in a small group living structure. Men come from various backgrounds and experiences, and the Phikeia must adjust to them all.

The Phikeia will find himself with men of various religious persuasions and differing ethical standards. In all this, every man will be challenged to reach a conclusion as to what is truly a "good" for all—behaviors which will rest upon that which is both true and good.

Fraternity living brings a closeness that one would not experience in dormitory living. It is broader than one would find in apartment living with two or three others.

A moral way of life is not listing things that are "sins" and then avoiding those things. It is in college that one is challenged to establish an adult moral life—a life which sets aside religion based upon rigid rules and moves into a positive and ever-deepening search for union with others where the morality of one seeks the good of the other.

In a way, the value of rectitude is that aspect of fraternity living which makes a constant demand that we love others. There is much more to it than a vertical relationship with God. There is a reaching out to other people—a concern for others—that eliminates no one. Rectitude is really an adult response to love and it is at the same time a rejection of egocentrism and narcissism.

Rectitude says that as a fraternity man "I have passed from the world of being a child to the world of being an adult. I wish another well. I have this desire so strongly in myself that I will never do anything which would harm the other person." A commitment to rectitude is a consistent demand to act responsibly and lovingly during one's college days and throughout life.

Questions

1. List the three cardinal principles of Phi Delta Theta and describe how they apply in daily life.
2. From what document do these principles come?
3. Who articulated the principles as we know them today?
4. What is the Athenian ideal of friendship?
5. Why are we "our brothers' keepers?"
6. Why is scholarship important to membership in Phi Delta Theta?
7. What is the Fraternity's role in the scholarship performance of its members?
8. What is rectitude?
9. In what occupation did most of the Founders serve?
10. How does the Phikeia oath apply to the Three Principles?

Essays

1. Give a personal definition of friendship.
2. What is your idea of scholarship excellence?
3. Discuss your moral principles. What is most important to you morally? What are the values and ethics of your fellow Phikeias?

III

I believe in the college fraternity, creator of friendships.
I believe in its quick sympathies, and its helping hand.
I believe in its brave idealism,
stirring every valiant emotion,
rousing every potential talent.
I believe in its compelling drive
for scholarship,
for genuine culture,
for clear-eyed honesty,
for business integrity.
I believe in the college fraternity, maker of men.
ARTHUR R. PRIEST, DEPAUW 1891

History of Greek Societies

THE FIRST Greek-letter organization was Phi Beta Kappa founded December 5, 1776, at the College of William and Mary in Williamsburg, Virginia, the second-oldest institution for higher learning in America. The Flat Hat Club, a secret society which was literary and social in nature but not Greek had preceded Phi Beta Kappa by 26 years. Phi Beta Kappa had all the characteristics of today's fraternities: a secret motto, a ritual, a grip, a badge, principles of high idealism, a bond of friendship and camaraderie, and an urge to share the organization's values through expansion to other campuses. The society was formed for social as well as literary purposes and held regular meetings in which members discussed highly charged and controversial subjects such as taxation and freedom. In this period of revolution, these debates could only be held secretly. In December, 1779, the parent chapter authorized the establishment of chapters at Yale and Harvard, and in January, 1781, as the British and American armies battled along the Virginia peninsula, it ceased its own operations.

The chapter at Yale was to be called Zeta, but when it was actually established, November 13, 1780, it took the name Alpha of Connecticut. Similarly, the Harvard chapter called itself Alpha of Massachusetts when it was established September 5, 1781. These two chapters together organized a chapter at Dartmouth in 1787, and there was no further expansion for thirty years, until the Alpha of New York was established at Union College.

Owing to the prejudice against secret societies aroused by the anti-Masonic sentiment, which began in 1826 when a bitter Freemason, William Morgan, disappeared after threatening to expose the secrets of the Masonic Fraternity, the Harvard chapter revealed the secrets of Phi Beta Kappa in 1831. It was exposed that the Greek letters, ΦBK, were the initials of *Φιλοσοφια Βιου Κυβερνητη*, meaning, "Philosophy is the guide of life." Soon afterward, Phi

Facing Page: Archived mural at Miami University depicts the Great Snowball Rebellion, the founding of the Miami Triad fraternities, and other historical events at Miami.

Beta Kappa became strictly an honor society whose membership recognized scholastic achievement. Today, Phi Beta Kappa is the most prestigious honor society in North America.

Inspired by the Phi Beta Kappas at Union College in Schenectady, New York, students formed the Kappa Alpha Society. The new fraternity was much like Phi Beta Kappa except that its purpose was social more than literary. Although the faculty opposed the new society, students embraced the new fraternity and founded two more Greek organizations: Sigma Phi on March 4, 1827, and Delta Phi on November 17, 1827. Together these three fraternities formed the "Union Triad" and were the basis for the expansion of the American college fraternity.

THE OLD RALEIGH TAVERN
Williamsburg, Virginia, where Phi Beta Kappa was founded in 1776.

Sigma Phi was the first of the Union Triad to establish a branch organization when it placed its Beta chapter at Hamilton College in 1831. One year later, Alpha Delta Phi was founded by the students at Hamilton to rival the Sigma Phis. In November, 1833, Psi Upsilon was formed at Union, and that same year Kappa Alpha established a chapter at Williams College in Williamsburg, Massachusetts, being followed one year later on that campus by Sigma Phi. At Williams the fraternities found a new rival in the form of an anti-secret society called the Social Fraternity which later united with similar organizations to form Delta Upsilon in 1834. Alpha Delta Phi made a bold move in 1833 by establishing its second chapter at Miami University in Oxford, Ohio, which was the Far West at that time. This was the first chapter of any fraternity west of the Allegheny Mountains.

In 1839, Beta Theta Pi was founded at Miami University by students who, after a quarrel with the Alpha Delta Phis, believed that a fraternal society could be a vehicle for moral and intellectual growth. Beta Theta Pi thus became the first fraternity *founded* west of the Alleghenies.

In protest against the current president of the University, students of Miami blocked the entrances of the main educational and administrative building in the winter of 1847 in what came to be known as the Great Snowball Rebellion. The president, determined to suppress the uprising, expelled a majority of the student body, among them nearly all of the members of the only two fraternities on campus. On December 26, 1848, Phi Delta Theta was founded, and was the first fraternity aside from the venerable Phi Beta Kappa to be founded on a campus without a Greek-letter organization. Sigma Chi was formed in 1855 from one faction of a divided Delta Kappa Epsilon chapter at Miami University. Together, Beta Theta Pi, Phi Delta Theta, and Sigma Chi form the "Miami Triad." The importance of the triad comes from the expansion of these three fraternities throughout the West and South, making them the first truly national Greek organizations.

The Civil War interrupted most fraternity operations, and as Americans chose sides in the United States' most devastating war, fraternity brothers often found themselves pitted against each other. Fraternity bonds, however, often accounted for many prisoners being exchanged or given better treatment. Only one fraternity was founded during this time, Theta Xi at Rensselaer Polytechnic Institute.

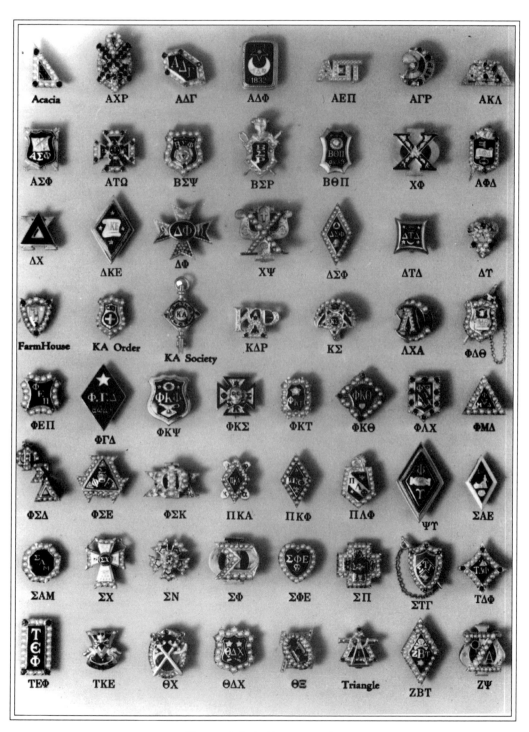

VARIOUS MEN'S FRATERNITY BADGES

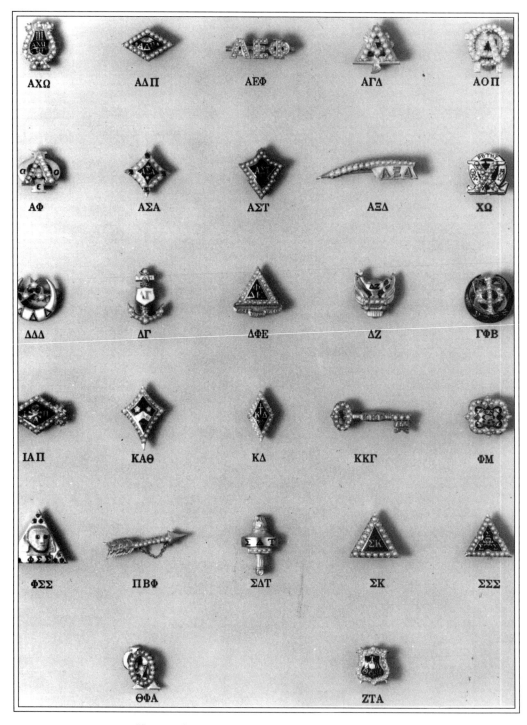

AΧΩ ΑΔΠ ΑΕΦ ΑΓΔ ΑΟΠ

ΑΦ ΑΣΑ ΑΣΤ ΑΞΔ ΧΩ

ΔΔΔ ΔΓ ΔΦΕ ΔΖ ΓΦΒ

ΙΑΠ ΚΑΘ ΚΔ ΚΚΓ ΦΜ

ΦΣΣ ΠΒΦ ΣΔΤ ΣΚ ΣΣΣ

ΘΦΑ ΖΤΑ

Various Sorority & Women's Fraternity Badges

After the war, northern fraternities were reluctant to expand to the South, so many southern Greek societies were founded during this period. Alpha Tau Omega was founded at the Virginia Military Institute in Lexington, Virginia in 1865, as were Kappa Sigma in 1869 and Sigma Nu in 1869. Across town at Washington & Lee University, Kappa Alpha Order was founded in 1865.

Other significant foundings are: Delta Chi in 1890, Tau Kappa Epsilon in 1899, Sigma Phi Epsilon in 1901, and Lambda Chi Alpha in 1909.

Although the majority of Greek-letter societies were founded between 1865 and 1900, more chapters were chartered in the 1900's than in the preceding century and a quarter. The American college fraternity rapidly spread to campuses across the United States and Canada.

Many obstacles appeared on the fraternities' road to progress, including two world wars, the Great Depression, and the socio-political upheaval of the 1960s, but fraternities have seen steady growth and now fraternity membership numbers nearly five million. Charges of hazing, alcohol abuse and anti-intellectualism have challenged Greek societies to emphasize community service, scholarship programming, and responsible social events.

Universities know, however, that fraternity members have a 65 to 70 percent graduation rate compared to 40 percent for nonmembers. The facts that fraternity members show more loyalty to their alma mater, are more involved as undergraduates and alumni, and make more donations to their schools offer a convincing case for the value and worth of Greek societies.

Women's groups

There are three firsts among women's fraternities. Alpha Delta Pi is counted as the first sisterhood, having been founded as the Adelphean Society in 1851. Pi Beta Phi came into being in 1867 as the first organization of college women established as a national college fraternity. Kappa Alpha Theta was organized in January, 1870, as the first Greek-letter society for women.

While there were scattered cases of women elected to the men's fraternities, it early became evident that there was a distinct field for similar organizations for women. For many years in schools for young women, societies bearing Greek or classical names were common, such as Adelphean, already named, Euterpean, and Philomathean. These became founding chapters of national bodies and claimed precedence by virtue of the initial dates of their parent local organizations.

The I.C. Sorosis, similar in purpose to the Greek-letter societies, was founded at Monmouth College in 1867. In 1870 at Indiana Asbury University, now DePauw, Kappa Alpha Theta was born. In the same year Kappa Kappa Gamma was established at Monmouth in Illinois. Alpha Phi originated at Syracuse University in New York in 1872, and in 1873 Delta Gamma began at the Lewis School for Young Women in Oxford, Mississippi. On November 9, 1874, Sigma Kappa was founded at Colby College in Waterville, Maine, and on November 11, Gamma Phi Beta followed Alpha Phi at Syracuse. Alpha Chi Omega was founded at DePauw University in 1885 and Delta Delta Delta was organized at Boston University in 1888. That same year, I.C. Sorosis officially adopted the Greek name Pi Beta Phi which it had used from the beginning as a secret motto.

Other women's sororities founded in the nineteenth century are Alpha Xi Delta in 1893 at Lombard College (now Knox) in Galesburg, Illinois; Chi Omega in 1895 at the University of Arkansas, Fayetteville; Alpha Omicron Pi in 1897 at Barnard College, New York City; Kappa Delta in 1897 at Longwood College, Farmville, Virginia; and Zeta Tau Alpha in 1898, also at

Prominent Greek Organizations

Founded	Organization	Chapters in 2000

Men's Fraternities

Founded	Organization	Chapters in 2000
1825	Kappa Alpha Society	9
1827	Sigma Phi	10
1827	Delta Phi	19
1832	Alpha Delta Phi	25
1833	Psi Upsilon	31
1834	Delta Upsilon	86
1839	Beta Theta Pi	139
1841	Chi Psi	32
1844	Delta Kappa Epsilon	62
1845	Alpha Sigma Phi	54
1847	Delta Psi	10
1847	Zeta Psi	50
1847	Theta Delta Chi	34
1848	Phi Gamma Delta	128
1848	Phi Delta Theta	173
1850	Phi Kappa Sigma	64
1852	Phi Kappa Psi	81
1854	Chi Phi	56
1855	Sigma Chi	228
1856	Sigma Alpha Epsilon	206
1856	Theta Chi	144
1858	Delta Tau Delta	117
1864	Theta Xi	53
1865	Alpha Tau Omega	157
1865	Kappa Alpha Order	131
1868	Pi Kappa Alpha	204
1869	Sigma Nu	204
1869	Kappa Sigma	224
1873	Phi Sigma Kappa	93
1889	Phi Kappa Theta	53
1890	Delta Chi	107
1895	Pi Lambda Phi	55
1895	Alpha Chi Rho	50
1897	Sigma Pi	123
1898	Zeta Beta Tau	26
1899	Tau Kappa Epsilon	268
1899	Delta Sigma Phi	109
1900	Kappa Delta Phi	15
1901	Sigma Phi Epsilon	239
1904	Alpha Gamma Rho	63
1904	Acacia	38
1904	Pi Kappa Phi	129
1905	Kappa Delta Rho	42

Founded	Organization	Chapters
1905	FarmHouse	27
1906	Phi Kappa Tau	84
1907	Triangle	32
1909	Lambda Chi Alpha	205
1909	Sigma Alpha Mu	70
1910	Tau Epsilon Phi	33
1910	Tau Delta Phi	6
1911	Kappa Alpha Psi	300
1913	Alpha Epsilon Pi	92
1914	Alpha Kappa Lambda	33
1914	Alpha Phi Delta	38
1918	Phi Mu Delta	11
1920	Sigma Tau Gamma	76
1922	Alpha Gamma Sigma	7
1924	Alpha Delta Gamma	12
1925	Phi Lambda Chi	9

Women's Fraternities & Sororities

Founded	Organization	Chapters
1851	Alpha Delta Pi	131
1852	Phi Mu	132
1867	Pi Beta Phi	129
1870	Kappa Alpha Theta	125
1870	Kappa Kappa Gamma	128
1872	Alpha Phi	147
1873	Delta Gamma	140
1874	Sigma Kappa	113
1884	Gamma Phi Beta	109
1885	Alpha Chi Omega	134
1888	Delta Delta Delta	132
1893	Alpha Xi Delta	110
1895	Chi Omega	174
1897	Alpha Omicron Pi	111
1897	Kappa Delta	124
1898	Sigma Sigma Sigma	106
1898	Zeta Tau Alpha	226
1899	Alpha Sigma Tau	62
1901	Alpha Sigma Alpha	74
1902	Delta Zeta	169
1904	Alpha Gamma Delta	112
1909	Alpha Epsilon Phi	49
1912	Theta Phi Alpha	25
1913	Phi Sigma Sigma	113
1917	Delta Phi Epsilon	89
1917	Sigma Delta Tau	59

Longwood. Two other women's fraternities were founded at Longwood College: Sigma Sigma Sigma in 1898 and Alpha Sigma Alpha in 1901, but until 1947 they limited their chapters to teacher colleges. The National Panhellenic Conference was organized in 1902 and now includes twenty-six women's fraternities.

Two members of Phi Delta Theta have had the distinction of being uniquely honored by women's fraternities. In 1879, George Banta, Sr., *Franklin-Indiana 1876,* was initiated by Delta Gamma so that he could help Delta Gamma's expansion efforts in the Midwest.

In 1902, Guy Potter Benton, *Ohio Wesleyan 1886,* then president of Miami University, proposed to a few of his favorite students that they form a sorority with the intention that it become a national organization. He helped them write a constitution and ritual. For his help, the women made him grand patron of Delta Zeta. He was the only man ever allowed to wear the Delta Zeta pin.

Although it was common in the early days of Greek societies to have honorary members, these two men are held in special regard by these women's groups. Now, honorary and dual membership are both prohibited by most Greek-letter fraternities.

All of the women's groups were called fraternities in the beginning because no other word existed. Then in 1882, Gamma Phi Beta was named a "sorority," a coined word suggested by their advisor who was a professor of Latin, and who thought the word "fraternity" was ill-advised for a group of young ladies. However, the other Greek-letter societies for women had already been incorporated as fraternities, and in 1909 the National Panhellenic Conference revised its Constitution to use the word "fraternity" throughout. This usage still prevails.

The NIC and NPC

In the early days of fraternity expansion, there was a bitter rivalry between the various groups, not only for members but for recognition and prestige. The women's groups were better than the men's about fostering a sense of interfraternalism. In 1902, after several preliminary meetings, the seven women's fraternities met in Boston to form the National Panhellenic Conference (NPC). The conference's mission was to encourage an interfraternal spirit among the members, to establish better relations with host institutions and to provide service to members' chapters.

In 1909, the men's groups formed the North-American Interfraternity Conference (NIC) aimed at the same goals as the NPC. The men, too, had held several previous meetings to discuss cooperation versus inter-fraternal rivalry.

The NPHC

The first black Greek-letter men's fraternity, Alpha Phi Alpha, was established at Cornell University in 1906. Although it does not now limit its membership exclusively to African-Americans, Alpha Phi Alpha was first established as a social and intellectual society for black collegians. In 1911, Omega Psi Phi was founded at Howard University in Washington, D.C. Kappa Alpha Psi was founded at Indiana University in 1911, and Phi Beta Sigma was founded at Howard in 1914. Chapters of these four fraternities quickly spread to colleges and universities across the United States. Their purpose was to promote scholarship and moral standards, as well as to foster a sense of unity among black collegians and support civil rights.

Alpha Kappa Alpha, the first Greek-letter fraternity for black women, was founded in 1908 at Howard University. The organization was intended to promote scholastic achievement, ethical standards, and unity among its members. This founding was quickly followed by Delta Sigma Theta at Howard in 1913, Zeta Phi Beta at Howard in 1920, and Sigma Gamma Rho in Indianapolis in 1922.

In 1930, the National Pan-Hellenic Council

(NPHC) was founded to foster cooperation among all eight of the Greek-letter societies for African-American men and women. Today, the NPHC member groups no longer limit membership to blacks. The organization promotes community service programs, scholarship, educational programs and civil rights.

Honor and Recognition Societies
Although an initiated member is prohibited from being initiated into a similar society, that does not bar him from membership in honor or recognition societies. Honor societies are college associations whose membership confers honor for scholarship achievement, leadership, or other achievements. Typical college honor societies include Phi Beta Kappa, Mortar Board,

Phi Eta Sigma, Order of Omega, and Tau Beta Pi.

A professional fraternity is a specialized society that limits membership to a single vocational or professional field. Usually such fraternities are coeducational and can initiate members of general Greek societies. Examples are Delta Sigma Pi, business; Phi Delta Phi, law; Phi Chi, medicine; Phi Delta Kappa, education.

A recognition or departmental society confers membership in recognition of students' interests or achievements in a restrictive field of study. Examples include Alpha Phi Omega, campus service; Arnold Air Society, Air Force; Blue Key, student activities; Omicron Delta Kappa, leadership; and Pi Delta Phi, French.

THE OLD RALEIGH TAVERN AS IT APPEARS TODAY IN HISTORIC WILLIAMSBURG, VIRGINIA.

Questions

1. What was the first Greek-letter society and where and when was it founded?
2. What is the Union Triad?
3. What is the Miami Triad?
4. What is the NIC? The NPC? The NPHC?
5. What is the difference between honor, professional, and recognition societies? Give examples of each.
6. What is the first sisterhood? The first national college fraternity for women? The first Greek-letter society for women?
7. Who are the two members of Phi Delta Theta who were honored by women's fraternities?
8. What happened to Phi Beta Kappa in 1831?

Essays

1. Discuss the history of the Greek community on your campus. What was the first chapter? When was your chapter founded?
2. List the honor societies on your campus. Are any brothers or Phikeias members of these societies?

IV

History of Phi Delta Theta

THE FIRST FRATERNITY at Miami University was Alpha Delta Phi. This fraternity, founded at Hamilton College in 1832, placed its second chapter at Miami University in 1833. Thus, Miami was the fourth college to be entered by fraternities, and the first in the West. The importance of this move was such that it set the stage for the founding of the Miami Triad, three fraternities that substantially aided in the expansion of Greek societies across the United States and Canada.

The small nucleus of men composing Alpha Delta Phi had a reputation for good scholarship and citizenship. However, the fraternity, about which little was known, was regarded with suspicion by the professors and students. This society was the only Greek letter fraternity on campus until Beta Theta Pi was founded in 1839.

Friction between the fraternity and other students broke out when the Alpha Delta Phis

attempted to gain control of the two literary societies then on campus. Through the efforts of John Reily Knox and other members of the societies, a law was passed barring all members of Alpha Delta Phi from membership in either of the literary groups. Feeling against the fraternity ran so high that the president of Miami University, George Junkin, asked the board of trustees to compel the fraternity to disband. Upon due investigation it was found that the fraternity had done no wrong, nor was it operating at a disadvantage to the University. Immediately after this, President Junkin resigned from his office.

In 1839, John Reily Knox, who had so successfully fought the Greeks, saw that a fraternity was not the ruthless, haughty, and pompous organization that he had previously supposed. Its principles were of a most sound nature, he believed; but there were certain detrimental features brought out in the functioning of Alpha Delta Phi that could be successfully combated in the operation of any such similar organization.

Facing Page: Miami University as it appeared in 1835. This mural is displayed at General Headquarters in Oxford, Ohio.

On August 8, 1839, John Reily Knox and Samuel T. Marshall formulated the constitution, name, and motto of the first fraternity to be founded west of the Alleghenies, Beta Theta Pi. Very soon thereafter, J. G. Smith joined them. At first the Betas were very much in opposition to the Alphas, but because of the similarity of the groups, it was impossible for them to fight each other. In 1843, the two fraternities pledged mutual aid in fighting the growing antagonism of the faculty.

Until 1847, the fraternities existed under cover of secrecy. The members did not wear their pins on campus, nor make mention of the fraternities in any official capacity with the University. Dr. E. D. MacMaster was then president of Miami University, and on the night of January 12, 1848, the students staged the Great Snowball Rebellion in protest against his unpopular administration.

Huge balls of snow, broken furniture, and sticks of wood were packed tightly against the doors of the chapel and recitation rooms of the main building. Among the students engaged in this revolt were members of both Alpha Delta Phi and Beta Theta Pi. Some of the snow was removed the next day by the university, but that night the barricade was rebuilt even more strongly than before with more snow, stoves, tables, and cord wood added to the buttresses.

Quick action against the offenders was taken by Dr. MacMaster, and many of the culprits were expelled. Before the rebellion there had been eight Alphas and eight Betas at the University. The only two Alphas who were not expelled or did not leave after the rebellion departed after commencement. Three Betas remained, two of whom graduated at the commencement of 1848. Thus, with the arrival of the winter of 1848-1849, there were no fraternities

"The Immortal Six"

ROBERT
MORRISON

JOHN McMILLAN
WILSON

ROBERT THOMPSON
DRAKE

JOHN WOLFE
LINDLEY

ARDIVAN WALKER
RODGERS

ANDREW WATTS
ROGERS

on campus, and only one Greek at Miami.

In the fall of 1848, Robert Morrison, a senior, proposed to fellow classmate, John McMillan Wilson, that they organize a Greek-letter society. Two juniors, Robert Thompson Drake and John Wolfe Lindley, and two sophomores, Ardivan Walker Rodgers and Andrew Watts Rogers, were enlisted in the project. Phi Delta Theta was founded on December 26, 1848, in Wilson's room in the dormitory known then as Northeast Building or Old North Hall, now called Elliott Hall. Several subsequent meetings were held in the same room.

Four Historic Meetings

The six founders held three meetings on December 26, 28, and 30. On the 26th, they "resolve[d] that we constitute ourselves into a secret society," and appointed a committee to create a motto, bond, and constitution for the society. On the 28th, the report of the committee was considered and amended. On the 30th, the report was further debated and finally adopted. On January 1, 1849, Morton George Williams, the first man pledged to Phi Delta Theta, was initiated. The ceremony was followed by a banquet at an Oxford hotel.

Morrison and Wilson were the joint authors of The Bond of Phi Delta Theta, which is the fundamental law of the Fraternity. It has remained unchanged from that day to this. So far as is known, it is the only document of any fraternity of such a character, and it is easy to understand the veneration with which all Phis regard it. Morrison signed The Bond first, Wilson next, and then the others. Morrison and Wilson likewise determined the name of the society upon the basis of the secret Greek motto, selected by Morrison, who was an excellent Greek scholar. Morrison designed the shield form of the badge, with the eye as an emblem, while Wilson suggested the scroll.

It is worth noting how well these men did their work. The Bond remains unchanged to this day; the badge is essentially unchanged; the Articles of Union served, with minor amendments, until 1880 and their fundamental laws are still embodied in the Constitution and General Statutes.

In 1851, shortly before the Alphas and Betas returned to the Miami campus, Benjamin Harrison was president of the Ohio Alpha Chapter of Phi Delta Theta. It was then that a faction of sympathizers in the Fraternity objected to the expulsion of J. H. Childs and J. G. McNutt for refusing to heed the principles of The Bond after repeated warnings made to them by the chapter. As a result, H. Denny, S. R. Matthews, and A. C. Kemper withdrew from the Fraternity in protest against the action. Denny later joined the Alphas, and Childs, McNutt, Matthews and Kemper became charter members of the Kappa Chapter of Delta Kappa Epsilon at Miami. Forty-six years later, Kemper was readmitted to Phi Delta Theta, having resigned from Delta Kappa Epsilon.

In 1854, strife within the chapter of Delta Kappa Epsilon crystallized during an all-campus election campaign. Whitelaw Reid, then president of the chapter, believed that the fraternity should vote as a body so as to elect the fraternity's candidate to office. The fraternity was evenly divided until feeling rose so high that six men, T. C. Bell, J. P. Caldwell, D. W. Cooper, I. M. Jordan, B. P. Runkle, and F. H. Scobey withdrew, leaving behind the charter, records, and seals. This group, together with a seventh man, W. L. Lockwood, on June 28, 1855, founded a new fraternity, Sigma Phi.

This new fraternity was beset with difficulties in its formation. The founders did not know that there was already an organization by the same name in the East, and someone made off with the ritual and initiation properties of the fraternity. In January, 1856, the seven men adopted a new constitution, grand seal, and badge, and elected to call their fraternity Sigma Chi.

Thus were Phi Delta Theta, Beta Theta Pi, and Sigma Chi founded at Miami University and became known as the Miami Triad.

The Immortal Six

The six founders were men of strong character, deep conviction, and unusual ability. All completed their college courses, most of them with distinction. As was the custom of the time, each received the M. A. degree three years later.

At the time of the founding, their ages ranged from twenty-three to twenty-seven years; all of them were sufficiently mature to know what should be the objects of an ideal brotherhood, and to formulate well-considered plans for its government.

Robert Morrison

Robert Morrison, the grandson of a Continental soldier of the same name, was born March 15, 1822, on a farm in Greene County, Pennsylvania. Most of his childhood was spent on a farm near Mount Gilead, Ohio. He walked three miles to and from school daily, and seven miles to church on Sundays. He entered Ohio University at Athens in 1839, and completed two years of schooling. He taught school for several years, and then entered Miami University in the spring of 1846. After graduation in 1849 he attended the Associated Reformed Theological Seminary in Oxford, taught school for a brief period, and received a license to preach after attending the New Albany, Indiana, Presbyterian Theological Seminary. From 1854 until 1868 he preached and edited religious newspapers in and about Louisville, Kentucky. He was principal of an academy at Waterford, Knox County, Ohio. From 1875 to 1900, he organized churches and missions, and did domestic mission work in Missouri. From 1879 to 1881, he succeeded in liquidating the debt of Westminster College. In 1897, he received the degree of Doctor of Divinity from Miami. He retired to a farm near Fulton, Missouri, in 1900, where he died July 27,

1902, at the age of 80. Throughout his life, he manifested an active interest in the Fraternity, attending many of the Conventions, including the Semi-Centennial in Columbus, Ohio, in 1898.

Morrison's philosophy is best expressed by what he termed his guiding principle, "To do what ought to be done but what would not have been done unless I did it, I thought to be my duty." His life work involved hardship, self-denial, and sacrifice, and he did much to advance the cause of education and the church.

John McMillan Wilson

Brother Wilson was born September 10, 1825, on a farm in Union County, Indiana. He attended Xenia Academy, and entered Miami University in 1846. He received an A.B. degree in 1849 and an M.A. degree in 1852. From 1849 until 1854, he taught part of the time at the Western Female Seminary and attended the theological seminary in Oxford intermittently. In 1855, he became pastor of the church at Morning Sun, Ohio. During the Civil War, he was commissioned as a recruiting officer in both Ohio and

MONUMENT TO ROBERT MORRISON
Erected at his grave in Fulton, Missouri, 1904.

Indiana. After the war, he went to Southern Illinois where he was engaged in various enterprises. He died July 19, 1874, in Benton, Illinois. During his residence near Oxford, he exercised a watchful eye over the society he had helped found and was known to the undergraduates as "Pop" Wilson.

Robert Thompson Drake

Brother Drake was born in Clark County, Ohio, March 6, 1822. He graduated from Miami University in 1850 and the New Albany Presbyterian Theological Seminary in 1853. While at the latter institution, he taught mathematics and natural philosophy in Anderson's Female Seminary. He attended Princeton Theological Seminary 1854–55 as a graduate student, and he was ordained by the presbytery of Des Moines in 1857. He preached at churches in Iowa, Indiana, Kentucky, and Ohio. He died March 19, 1873, in New Castle, Indiana, and was buried at Lebanon, Ohio.

John Wolfe Lindley

John Wolfe Lindley was born August 23, 1826, near Fredericktown, Knox County, Ohio. He was a third cousin of Robert Morrison. He received his A.B. degree from Miami in 1850 and his M.A. degree in 1853. He taught in schools in New Hagerstown, Ohio; Richmond, Ohio; Charleston, Indiana; Paducah, Kentucky, and subsequently settled down as a farmer near Fredricktown, Ohio, in 1862. He became a justice of the peace in 1868. He attended many of the Fraternity Conventions, among them the Semi-Centennial celebration in 1898 and the General Convention at New York in 1902. He died December 16, 1907, age 81, the last surviving founder.

Ardivan Walker Rodgers

Ardivan Walker Rodgers was born in Miami County, near Piqua, Ohio, October 20, 1824, the great-grandson of a Revolutionary War captain

and the grandson of a captain in the War of 1812. He received an A.B. degree in 1851 and an M.A. degree in 1854. He attended the Seminary at Oxford briefly, and then taught school, studying during his five years of teaching for the United Presbyterian ministry. He died from typhoid fever, December 11, 1856, at Brighton, Iowa, where he had gone to visit his father. He was the first of the founders to die.

Andrew Watts Rogers

Andrew Watts Rogers entered Miami University in the preparatory school in 1846, and graduated with an A.B. degree in 1851, receiving an M.A. degree in 1854. He taught school and was admitted to the bar in Tennessee. He moved to Illinois in 1858 and began active legal practice there, coming in contact with Abraham Lincoln and Stephen A. Douglas. He was a major in the Union army in the battles around Jackson, Mississippi. He served as lieutenant-colonel during

FOUNDERS PLAQUE
Exterior of Elliott Hall, installed 1899.

the assault of Vicksburg, and was in command of the 81st Illinois Voluntary Infantry, when it was the last to leave the field during the Battle of Guntown. He was later colonel of the regiment, and led the assault on the Spanish fort on Dauphin Island in Mobile Bay.

He resumed his law practice in Missouri, serving as special judge and member of the state legislature. He later edited the Warrensburg Journal-Democrat, and was commander of the Colonel Grover Post of the G.A.R. He married Sallie Matthews, daughter of Professor Matthews of the Miami University faculty and sister of Associate Justice Stanley Matthews of the United States Supreme Court. Colonel Rogers died December 26, 1901, in Warrensburg, Missouri.

Expansion and Growth

The first branch of Phi Delta Theta was established October 11, 1849, at Indiana University. The Indiana Chapter has the longest continuous existence of any in the Fraternity. The third chapter was chartered at Centre College by Morton George Williams, the first initiate, who had transferred there. He died in September 1851, and Wilson referred to him as "the first chosen, the first taken, and the best beloved." Indiana Beta was established in November 1850, at Wabash College, by Robert Gaston Elliott, one of the charter members of Indiana Alpha. The next four chapters, Ohio Gamma Prime, at Wittenburg; Texas Alpha Prime, at Austin; Kentucky Beta, at the Kentucky Military Institute; and Kentucky Gamma, at Georgetown, survived only a brief time.

From April to November 1852, a second chapter, the Ohio Beta, existed at Miami, and for a few months in 1855 two chapters also existed at Centre. These are the only known instances of a fraternity chartering two chapters on one campus. During this time the Miami chapter numbered among its presidents David

Swing, the great liberal minister, and Benjamin Harrison, general, governor, and president of the United States. In 1857, the parent chapter at Miami was suspended due to the graduation of all but one of its members.

The Dark Days of the War

The Civil War not only arrested development of the Fraternity, but caused the suspension of the chapters at Franklin, Ohio Wesleyan, Northwestern, Wisconsin, and Lawrence, leaving active chapters only at Indiana, Wabash, Butler and Centre. New chapters were installed in 1864 at Michigan, in 1865 at Chicago, and in 1868 at DePauw, Ohio University, and Hanover.

In its third decade, 1869–79, the Fraternity entered many Southern institutions, and in its fourth decade, 1879–89, it established chapters in Eastern institutions, making itself national in extent. The Lombard chapter was formed in 1878 from the parent and the only surviving chapter of Phi Sigma. It passed out of existence as a separate chapter when Lombard College in 1930 was absorbed by Knox College and the Lombard chapter was combined with the Knox chapter under the title of Illinois Delta-Zeta.

All the attendant members of the Centre chapter were graduated in 1879, but the chapter was continued by the absorption, in the fall, of the Centre chapter of one of the last remaining chapters of Delta Kappa. In 1885 the active members of the W.W.W., or Rainbow chapters, at the University of Texas, were initiated into the chapter of Phi Delta Theta there. Phi Delta Theta was established at Southwestern University by initiating the members of the Southwestern chapter of W.W.W. These two chapters had disagreed with the others in regard to the policy of uniting with Delta Tau Delta.

Kentucky Delta was established at Central University in 1885. In 1901, Centre College and Central University were consolidated under the former name, and the chapters at the two institutions were combined under the name of Kentucky Alpha-Delta. In 1887, Kappa Sigma Kappa, a fraternity having chapters in Virginia, disintegrated. Its chapters at Washington & Lee, Virginia Military Institute, Randolph-Macon, and Richmond united with Phi Delta Theta.

In 1865, an Indiana state convention was held at Indianapolis. It was the first state convention with chapter representation held by any fraternity. In addition, multi-province meetings were held annually in many areas.

In 1876, the first alumni club was organized at Franklin, Indiana. Charters have since been granted to alumni in Canada, Mexico, China, the Philippine Islands, and 49 States.

The chapter at the University of the South built the first house owned by Phi Delta Theta in 1884, the year after its establishment.

Fraternity Government

The original plan of government provided that the parent chapter at Miami should be the presiding chapter and should have the right to charter other chapters in Ohio as well as the first chapter in each other State of the Union. The first chapter in each State was granted the right to charter other chapters in the same State.

The presiding chapter was called the Grand Chapter until 1868, when an executive committee was established. It had a president, a secretary, and a varying number of members. In 1872, its powers were enlarged, and a grand banker was added. From 1876 to 1880, it was composed of a president, a secretary, a grand banker, and one member chosen by the national Grand Chapter. Until 1878, the first chapter in each state was the presiding chapter in that area and was called the state Grand Chapter. In 1880, the executive committee was changed to the General Council, composed of a president, a secretary, a treasurer, and a historian, and the

Fraternity was divided into provinces. Full executive powers were then conferred on the General Council. In 1896, an officer known as the reporter was added to the General Council. The five councilors constituted the board of trustees, which acted as a court of appeals to decide questions of legal concern. In 1922, the offices of secretary and historian were abolished and those two officers became members-at-

Minutes From The First Meeting.
This and other historic documents are kept in the archives at General Headquarters.

large of the General Council. In 1881, the Fraternity was incorporated under the laws of Ohio.

On December 1, 1947, the Fraternity completed and took occupancy of its impressive Memorial Library and General Headquarters Building in Oxford, Ohio. This memorial shrine, built in the tradition of Williamsburg and the tidewater country of Virginia, provides working quarters for an Executive Vice President and his staff; a spacious assembly room for conferences; an expansive library of more than 3,500 books and periodicals authored by and written about Phis; a room dedicated to the Founders, where items of memorabilia are displayed; and guest rooms to accommodate the officers and other members of the Fraternity from time to time. The memorial building was formally dedicated on September 4, 1948, at the celebration of Phi Delta Theta's centennial.

The Second Founders

During the two decades from 1870 to 1890, the growth of the Fraternity was very rapid, due principally to the efforts of Walter B. Palmer, *Emory-Vanderbilt 1877*, and George Banta, *Franklin-Indiana 1876*, for which they were given the title "Second Founders." George Banta was elected the first president of the General Council at the 1880 Convention. He also served as editor of the fourth and fifth editions of the Catalogue of Phi Delta Theta.

Walter B. Palmer was elected president of the General Council in 1896. He was the author of the HISTORY OF PHI DELTA THETA as well as the first MANUAL OF PHI DELTA THETA. He also served as the editor of THE SCROLL from 1883–1884.

It is worth noting that Phi Delta Theta has more chapters which are more than 100 years old than any other fraternity. These old and

THE OLD NORTH DORMITORY, CIRCA 1900.
The room to the left of the plaque was Wilson's. Morrison occupied the room directly below.

firmly established chapters help explain the great strength of the Fraternity in every section of the United States and Canada.

An International Fraternity

The first fraternity to expand into Canada was Zeta Psi. In 1879, it established a chapter at the University of Toronto. In 1883, Zeta Psi expanded to McGill University in Montréal, Quebec, and four other fraternities followed there, believing Canadian universities to be ripe for the expansion of Greek-letter societies.

In February, 1900, there came to the General Council an application signed by twelve students at McGill University. This overture from Canada was a total surprise and a very interesting one. But to extend Phi Delta Theta beyond the United States was a question for the entire Fraternity, and the McGill students were told that their request would be presented at the General Convention in November. Meanwhile, a Phi from Vermont made a visit to McGill and a member of Maine Alpha entered the Medical School there. At the November Convention in Louisville, these men recommended granting the charter, and after extended discussion the Convention voted for expansion into Canada. Quebec Alpha was installed April 5, 1902, by Phis from Dartmouth and Vermont. The ceremony took place in the Windsor Hotel with paraphernalia loaned from Dartmouth. It was an international celebration for a now international fraternity. At the installation banquet a toast to the King was followed by one to the President. Declared THE SCROLL, "The Phi Delta Thetas of McGill are thrice welcome: as fellow Americans, as college men, and as brothers in The Bond."

Phi Delta Theta continued to extend its presence in Canada. Canadian representation

THE SEMI-CENTENNIAL NATIONAL CONVENTION, COLUMBUS, OHIO, 1898.
Robert Morrison and John Wolfe Lindley appear in the center, front.

was extended from coast to coast when the Fraternity entered the University of Alberta, the University of British Columbia, Dalhousie University, and the University of Manitoba in 1930. Today, Phi Delta Theta has more chapters in Canada than any other fraternity.

The Fraternity Today

Phi Delta Theta now has more than 170 active chapters in 43 states and six Canadian provinces. The Fraternity has initiated nearly 190,000 men since 1848. More than 120 houses

"Second Founders"

GEORGE BANTA SR.   WALTER B. PALMER

for a total value of more than $50 million are owned by chartered house corporations. There are more than 90 recognized alumni clubs across the United States and Canada.

Phi Delta Theta is one of the foremost fraternities in establishing first chapters on campus. To date, 25 campuses have welcomed Phi Delta Theta as the pioneer fraternity, including Wittenberg, Austin, Kentucky Military Institute, Georgetown (Ky.), Wisconsin, Lawrence, Northwestern, Butler, Franklin, Indiana State, Nebraska, Vanderbilt, Central, Texas, Stanford, South Dakota, Whitman, Alberta, Willamette, Texas Tech, South Florida, Western Maryland, California at San Diego, University of Victoria, Ringling School of Art and Design, and McMaster.

Phi Delta Theta was the first to establish a day of celebration throughout the Fraternity when the third Wednesday of April was pronounced Alumni Day by the Convention of 1889. The Fraternity was the first to create an endowment for free lifetime subscriptions to the magazine, a plan later adopted by nearly every other fraternal organization. Phi Delta Theta was also the first to adopt a pledge pin and the first to publish a pledge manual. The first alumnus recognition button was also created by the Fraternity.

The first chapter of Phi Delta Theta to occupy a house was California Alpha. Tennessee Beta was the first chapter of Phi Delta Theta to own a house and the first fraternity to own a house in the South.

Phi Delta Theta members have occupied every major public office including the presidency and vice presidency of the United States, Speaker of the U.S. House of Representatives, U.S. Senators and Congressmen, State Governors and Senators in the Canadian House of Commons.

Leadership College

In 1987, the first Leadership College was held in Oxford, Ohio, with nearly 500 undergraduates in attendance. The first Leadership Colleges were held every two years on the off-years of the Biennial Convention. Now, the week-long College is held every year at Miami University, the birthplace of Phi Delta Theta.

Every chapter across the United States and Canada sends three or more representatives to participate in educational seminars, chapter meetings, and activities that heighten awareness of the issues that face the Fraternity today. The experience also builds a bond between Phis from different areas of the continent. Brothers have an opportunity to discuss topics of local and international concern, learn about leadership techniques and personal development.

Alumni and Greek professionals specializing in a variety of areas serve as faculty for the College.

Founders Day

Robert Morrison's birthday, March 15, was established in 1910 as Founders Day. Many alumni clubs and chapters meet on this date to honor the Founding Fathers and celebrate the occasion with ritualistic exercises.

Golden & Silver Legions

Members who have been Phis for 25 years are inducted into the Silver Legion. Members who have been Phis for 50 years are honored as Golden Legionnaires. Ceremonies inducting these alumni into the Legions are usually performed at Founders Day celebrations. Each legionnaire is given a pin acknowledging his years of devotion to the Fraternity.

Every five years after becoming a Golden Legionnaire, members are also honored as "Palladians." Palladians receive a charm inscribed with years since initiation, 55, 60, 65 or 70. Members who have been Phis for 75 or more years are Diamond Legionnaires.

Questions

1. What fraternities preceded Phi Delta Theta at Miami?
2. What was the Great Snowball Rebellion and what was its importance?
3. What fraternities existed at Miami University when Phi Delta Theta was founded?
4. Who first suggested the idea of the Fraternity and to whom?
5. What is the present name and the old name of the building in which Phi Delta Theta was founded?
6. What is The Bond and who composed it?
7. Who was "the first chosen, first taken and best beloved?"
8. What was the second chapter? The third?
9. Who were the "Second Founders?" What did they do?
10. How many chapters and members does Phi Delta Theta have today?
11. What was the first Phi Delta Theta chapter founded in Canada? When was it founded?

Essays

1. Give the dates and importance of each of the first four meetings of the Founders.
2. Give the names and background of each Founder.
3. Discuss how the Civil War affected the Fraternity.

V

The Organization

In the Fraternity's early years, Ohio Alpha, the parent chapter of the Fraternity, granted to the first chapter in each state, governing powers equal to those which the parent chapter itself enjoyed in the state of Ohio. The Alpha chapter in each state, called the State Grand Chapter, was thus given the right to grant charters within the state for establishment of new chapters. The first charter in a state could be granted only by the National Grand Chapter. Ohio Alpha exercised these powers of the National Grand Chapter until 1858 when they passed to Indiana Alpha. Subsequently they were in turn invested in Kentucky Alpha, Illinois Beta, Ohio Alpha, Ohio Delta, and Pennsylvania Alpha.

The first General Convention of the Fraternity was held in Cincinnati in 1851, when delegates from two chapters attended. From 1851 to 1878 inclusively, fifteen General Conventions

were held. These conventions had comparatively little power, although the Convention of 1868 created an Executive Committee to supervise the affairs of the Fraternity between Conventions. The Executive Committee sought to harmonize the constitutions of the various chapters so as to bring about uniformity and gradually build toward a common constitution for the Fraternity. In 1878, the Convention voted on charters for chapters and took this privilege away from the National Grand Chapter.

In many ways the Convention of 1880 was epoch-making and the most important to be held in the history of the Fraternity. The plan of government was overhauled, and the present system of a General Council and provinces was adopted. The State Grand Chapter and National Grand Chapter were abolished, the Executive Committee was discontinued, and the supreme power of the Fraternity was vested in the General Convention. To the General Council was delegated all executive and administrative functions between Conventions. As established by the Convention of 1880, the

General Council was made up of four officers, a president, secretary, treasurer, and historian. In 1896, a fifth member of the General Council, known as the reporter, was added.

The General Council was not again changed until 1922 when the offices of secretary and historian were abolished, and two members of the General Council who had previously held those offices were termed members-at-large. The other three members of the General Council, president, treasurer, and reporter, were designated as an Executive Committee of the General Council and vested with the authority to carry on Council business of a routine nature without the need of the votes of the other two.

In 1880, the chapters of the Fraternity were so few that only four provinces were necessary. The number of provinces was increased to seven in 1884, and now numbers nearly 50.

In 1918, the General Council employed an assistant to look after the growing work of correspondence and to centralize the keeping of records. He was headquartered in the Ohio Alpha Memorial Chapter House. The Convention of 1920 established a central office and created the position of executive secretary to have charge of it. The title was changed to Executive Vice President in 1972.

The central office of the Fraternity was moved to Detroit in 1923 and stayed there until 1926, when it returned to the birthplace of the Fraternity, Oxford, Ohio, In 1927, a building facing the Miami campus was purchased, but in 1941, this building was replaced with the current the memorial building. The Executive Vice President and his staff maintain their offices in this General Headquarters Building, which was dedicated during the celebration of the Centennial of the Fraternity, held September 1–5, 1948.

PHI DELTA THETA GENERAL HEADQUARTERS & MEMORIAL LIBRARY.
Dedicated in 1948 during the Fraternity's centennial in Oxford, Ohio, this is how the Paul E. Martin Building looks today. A new wing, seen to the left, was added in 1999.

General Convention

Since 1880, the General Convention has held all supreme and legislative powers of the Fraternity. The Convention, which meets every two years, has four main responsibilities and powers. They include:

- Electing the General Council;
- Revoking charters of chapters;
- Providing for the raising and disbursement of revenues;
- Enacting laws for the regulation of the Fraternity, since only the General Convention may amend the Ritual, Constitution, and General Statutes of the Fraternity.

One of the more important decisions a chapter makes is the selection of its delegate to the General Convention, because all formal action taken at the General Convention is the result of democratic voting, and it is typical for chapter delegates to constitute 65 to 75 percent of the total vote. Those with voting privileges at the Convention include:

- Undergraduate chapter delegates;
- Members of the General Council;
- Past Presidents of the General Council;
- Province Presidents;
- Survey Commissioners;
- The Executive Vice President;
- The Housing Commissioner;
- Other commissioners that the General Council may appoint;
- Alumni club delegates.

Volunteer Structure

All power and responsibility in Phi Delta Theta flows from the General Convention through an extensive volunteer and staff organization which manages the affairs of the Fraternity on an ongoing basis. Every facet of this organization plays some role in supporting the undergraduate chapters. The following descriptions highlight the primary responsibilities of each position.

The General Council: The General Convention elects a president and four additional members of the General Council whose responsibility it is to act as the executive and administrative board of the Fraternity, overseeing the affairs of Phi Delta Theta between Conventions. The Council interprets and executes all laws of the Fraternity, making such ordinances and appointments as it may deem necessary to promote the general welfare of Phi Delta Theta.

The Province President: For administrative purposes the chapters of the Fraternity are divided into geographical subdivisions called provinces. Each province is assigned a president who is a Phi Delta Theta alumnus volunteering his service to the Fraternity. The Province President is appointed to a two-year term of office by the General Council subject to the approval of the chapters in the respective area. The role of the Province President is to serve as a deputy of the General Council in safeguarding the welfare of the Fraternity in the section committed to his care. The Province President appoints chapter advisers, assists in the expansion of the Fraternity in his area, and makes visits to each chapter when necessary to work with the chapter officers, encouraging and assisting in the success of individual chapters.

The Chapter Advisory Board: Upon the chapter advisory board chairman rests one of the weightiest responsibilities in the whole scheme of the Fraternity's organization and administration. Selected by the Province President to serve a two-year term, this alumnus volunteer works with the officers and members of an individual chapter to help it maintain the high standards of Phi Delta Theta. The chapter advisory board chairman visits the chapter frequently and often attends committee, Phikeia, and chapter meetings. He is a guide, a counsellor, and a resource for the undergraduates. He is also chairman of the chapter's advisory board.

While the positions of Province President

and chapter adviser are organized to have a great deal of interaction with individual chapters, there exists in Phi Delta Theta a large cadre of alumni volunteers who serve on commissions and foundations organized to address specific issues and manage certain endowments within Phi Delta Theta.

The Survey Commission: The Survey Commission is composed of alumni volunteers, appointed by the General Council to two-year terms, and responsible for the location and creation of new chapters of the Fraternity. The commissioners investigate inquiries from four-year colleges and universities interested in the Fraternity's expansion to their campuses. In addition, the Survey Commission actively pursues opportunities to expand the Fraternity to campuses on which Phi Delta Theta would wish to be located.

The commission, in conjunction with the Headquarters staff, establishes interest groups and recommends the establishment of colonies and chapters to the General Council.

The Housing Commission: The Housing Commission is responsible for coordinating programs through the local housing corporations that promote safe, affordable housing for the chapters. Fire safety, insurance, property care, and risk management are a few of the areas with which the commission deals.

The Phi Delta Theta Educational Foundation: The 1958 General Convention adopted legislation for the establishment of a Phi Delta Theta Educational Foundation to provide for the advancement of learning. The trustees of the Educational Foundation award annual scholarships and fund the educational programs of the Fraternity. Since the beginning of the scholarship

The General Council, 2004-2006

MICHAEL G. SCARLATELLI
Kettering '76
President

RUDY M. PORCHIVINA
San Jose State '89
Treasurer

MARK H. OCHSENBEIN
Eastern Kentucky '77
Reporter

M. SCOTT MIETCHEN
Utah '84
Member-at-Large

CHRIS LAPPLE
California State-Northridge '80
Member-at-Large

The Roll of the Chapters

Italics indicate a revoked charter.

1. Ohio Alpha .... Miami 1848
2. Indiana Alpha .... Indiana 1849
3. Kentucky Alpha-Delta .... Centre 1850
4. Indiana Beta .... Wabash 1850
5. *Ohio Gamma Prime* .... *Wittenberg* *1852–1854*
6. *Texas Alpha Prime* .... *Austin* *1853–1854*
7. *Kentucky Beta* .... *Ky. Military Inst.* *1854–1856*
8. *Kentucky Gamma* .... *Georgetown* *1857–1876*
9. Wisconsin Alpha .... Wisconsin 1857
10. Wisconsin Beta .... Lawrence 1859
11. Illinois Alpha .... Northwestern 1859
12. Indiana Gamma .... Butler 1859
13. Ohio Beta .... Ohio Wesleyan 1860
14. Indiana Delta .... Franklin 1860
15. Indiana Epsilon .... Hanover 1861
16. Michigan Alpha .... Michigan 1864–1998
17. Illinois Beta .... Chicago 1865
18. Indiana Zeta .... DePauw 1868
19. Ohio Gamma .... Ohio 1868
20. Indiana Eta .... Indiana State 1869
21. *Virginia Alpha* .... *Roanoke* *1869–1896*
22. Missouri Alpha .... Missouri 1870
23. *Illinois Gamma* .... *Monmouth* *1871–1884*
24. Illinois Delta-Zeta .... Knox 1871
25. *Georgia Alpha Prime* .... *Oglethorpe* *1871–1872*
26. Georgia Alpha .... Georgia 1871
27. Georgia Beta .... Emory 1871
28. Iowa Alpha .... Iowa Wesleyan 1871
29. Georgia Gamma .... Mercer 1872
30. *Ohio Delta* .... *Wooster* *1872–1897*
31. New York Alpha .... Cornell 1872
32. *Pennsylvania Alpha* .... *Lafayette* *1873–1993*
33. California Alpha .... California 1873
34. Michigan Beta .... Michigan State 1873
35. Virginia Beta .... Virginia 1873
36. Virginia Gamma .... Randolph-Macon 1874
37. Ohio Epsilon .... Akron 1875
38. Nebraska Alpha .... Nebraska 1875
39. Virginia Delta .... Richmond 1875
40. Pennsylvania Beta .... Gettysburg 1875
41. Pennsylvania Gamma .... Washington & Jefferson 1875
42. Tennessee Alpha .... Vanderbilt 1876
43. Pennsylvania Eta .... Lehigh 1876
44. *Missouri Beta Prime* .... *Central* *1876–1878*
45. Mississippi Alpha .... Mississippi 1877
46. Alabama Alpha .... Alabama 1877
47. *Virginia Epsilon* .... *Virginia Military Inst.* *1878–1889*
48. *Illinois Epsilon* .... *Illinois Wesleyan* *1878–1897*
49. North Carolina Alpha .... Duke 1878
50. *Texas Alpha* .... *Trinity* *1878–1883*
51. *Illinois Zeta* † .... *Lombard* *1878*
52. Alabama Beta .... Auburn 1879–1993
53. *South Carolina Alpha* .... *Wofford* *1879–1885*
54. Pennsylvania Delta .... Allegheny 1879
55. Vermont Alpha .... Vermont 1879
56. Pennsylvania Epsilon .... Dickinson 1880
57. Missouri Beta .... Westminster 1880
58. *Minnesota Alpha* .... *Minnesota* *1881–1994*
59. Iowa Beta .... Iowa 1882
60. South Carolina Beta .... South Carolina 1882–2000
61. Kansas Alpha .... Kansas 1882

62. *Michigan Gamma* .... *Hillsdale* *1882–1898*
63. Tennessee Beta .... Sewanee 1883
64. Ohio Zeta .... Ohio State 1883
65. Texas Beta .... Texas 1883
66. Pennsylvania Zeta .... Pennsylvania 1883
67. New York Beta .... Union 1883
68. *New York Gamma* .... *C.C.N.Y.* *1884–1891*
69. *Maine Alpha* .... *Colby* *1884–1986*
70. *New York Delta* .... *Columbia* *1884–1935*
71. *New Hampshire Alpha* .... *Dartmouth* *1884–1960*
72. North Carolina Beta .... North Carolina 1885
73. Kentucky Delta ‡ .... Central 1885
74. *Massachusetts Alpha* .... *Williams* *1886–1966*
75. Texas Gamma .... Southwestern 1886
76. *Alabama Gamma* .... *Southern* *1887–1896*
77. *New York Epsilon* .... *Syracuse* *1887–1994*
78. Virginia Zeta .... Washington & Lee 1887
79. *Massachusetts Beta* .... *Amherst* *1888–1956*
80. *Rhode Island Alpha* .... *Brown* *1889–1968*
81. *Louisiana Alpha* .... *Tulane* *1889–1970*
82. Missouri Gamma .... Washington 1891
83. California Beta .... Stanford 1891
84. Indiana Theta .... Purdue 1893
85. Illinois Eta .... Illinois 1893
86. Ohio Eta .... Case Western Res. 1896
87. Ohio Theta .... Cincinnati 1898
88. Washington Alpha .... Washington 1900
89. Kentucky Epsilon .... Kentucky 1901
90. Quebec Alpha .... McGill 1902
91. Colorado Alpha .... Colorado 1902
92. Georgia Delta .... Georgia Tech 1902
93. Pennsylvania Theta .... Penn State 1904
94. Ontario Alpha .... Toronto 1906
95. South Dakota Alpha .... South Dakota 1906
96. Idaho Alpha .... Idaho 1908
97. Kansas Beta .... Washburn 1910
98. Oregon Alpha .... Oregon 1912–2000
99. *Colorado Beta* .... *Colorado College* *1913–1995*
100. Iowa Gamma .... Iowa State 1913
101. North Dakota Alpha .... North Dakota 1913
102. Ohio Iota .... Denison 1914
103. Washington Beta .... Whitman 1914
104. Utah Alpha .... Utah 1914
105. Oregon Beta .... Oregon State 1918
106. Washington Gamma .... Washington State 1918–2000
107. Pennsylvania Iota .... Pittsburgh 1918–1997
108. New York Zeta .... Colgate 1918
109. Oklahoma Alpha .... Oklahoma 1918
110. *Pennsylvania Kappa* .... *Swarthmore* *1918–1958*
111. Montana Alpha .... Montana 1920
112. Kansas Gamma .... Kansas State 1920
113. Colorado Gamma .... Colorado State 1920
114. Arizona Alpha .... Arizona 1922
115. Texas Delta .... Southern Methodist 1922
116. Florida Alpha .... Florida 1924
117. *California Gamma* .... *U.C.L.A.* *1924*
118. West Virginia Alpha .... West Virginia 1926
119. N. Carolina Gamma .... Davidson 1928
120. Alberta Alpha .... Alberta 1930
121. Manitoba Alpha .... Manitoba 1930
122. British Columbia Alpha .... British Columbia 1930
123. Maryland Alpha .... Maryland 1930
124. Nova Scotia Alpha .... Dalhousie 1930
125. Massachusetts Gamma ...... M.I.T. 1932

† Merged with Illinois Delta, 1930.
‡ Merged with Kentucky Alpha, 1901.

program, more than 1,200 scholarships with a total value of more than $2.2 million have been awarded. The total assets of the Foundation totals more than $10 million.

The Canadian Scholarship Foundation: The Canadian Scholarship Foundation was organized in 1973 to provide scholarships to Phi Delta Theta undergraduates on Canadian campuses. Since the beginning of the Canadian Scholarship Foundation, more than $85,000 in scholarships has been awarded.

The Frank J. R. Mitchell Fund: At the Convention of 1908, Frank J. R. Mitchell, the editor and manager of The Scroll, suggested a plan for life subscriptions which would in time provide adequate support for The Scroll. In 1910, he placed before the Convention a proposal, without precedent in the fraternity world, which called for a plan providing for a life payment of

ten dollars for each initiate. The principal of this fund now amounts to more than $4 million. Almost every fraternity and sorority has since adopted the plan of life subscription which Phi Delta Theta gave to the fraternity world.

The Convention of 1938 provided that, in Brother Mitchell's memory, the endowment should thenceforth be named the Frank J. R. Mitchell Scroll Endowment Fund.

The Walter B. Palmer Foundation: Finding that the endowment idea was sound, the General Council thought it appropriate to establish in 1922 an endowment in honor of Walter B. Palmer who had devoted his life to Fraternity service. The fund is known as the Walter B. Palmer Foundation. The principal is used for investment loans to assist chapter house corporations in purchasing, constructing, or refurbishing chapter houses. The principal of the Walter

THE CONVENTION HALL.
The 1948 Centennial Convention in Oxford, Ohio. Delegates are seated by province. Members of the General Council are seated behind the speakers' platform.

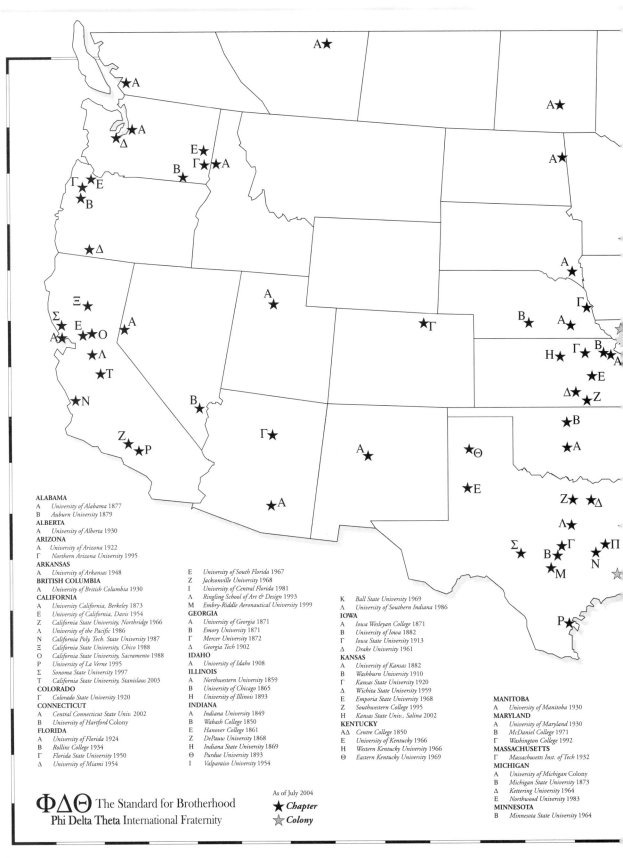

ALABAMA
A   *University of Alabama* 1877
B   *Auburn University* 1879

ALBERTA
A   *University of Alberta* 1930

ARIZONA
A   *University of Arizona* 1922
Γ   *Northern Arizona University* 1995

ARKANSAS
A   *University of Arkansas* 1948

BRITISH COLUMBIA
A   *University of British Columbia* 1930

CALIFORNIA
A   *University California, Berkeley* 1873
E   *University of California, Davis* 1954
Z   *California State University, Northridge* 1966
Λ   *University of the Pacific* 1986
N   *California Poly. Tech. State University* 1987
Ξ   *California State University, Chico* 1988
O   *California State University, Sacramento* 1988
P   *University of La Verne* 1995
Σ   *Sonoma State University* 1997
T   *California State University, Stanislaus* 2003

COLORADO
Γ   *Colorado State University* 1920

CONNECTICUT
A   *Central Connecticut State Univ.* 2002
B   *University of Hartford Colony*

FLORIDA
A   *University of Florida* 1924
B   *Rollins College* 1934
Γ   *Florida State University* 1950
Δ   *University of Miami* 1954
E   *University of South Florida* 1967
Z   *Jacksonville University* 1968
I   *University of Central Florida* 1981
Λ   *Ringling School of Art & Design* 1993
M   *Embry-Riddle Aeronautical University* 1999

GEORGIA
A   *University of Georgia* 1871
B   *Emory University* 1871
Γ   *Mercer University* 1872
Δ   *Georgia Tech* 1902

IDAHO
A   *University of Idaho* 1908

ILLINOIS
A   *Northwestern University* 1859
B   *University of Chicago* 1865
H   *University of Illinois* 1893

INDIANA
A   *Indiana University* 1849
B   *Wabash College* 1850
E   *Hanover College* 1861
Z   *DePauw University* 1868
H   *Indiana State University* 1869
Θ   *Purdue University* 1893
I   *Valparaiso University* 1954
K   *Ball State University* 1969
Λ   *University of Southern Indiana* 1986

IOWA
A   *Iowa Wesleyan College* 1871
B   *University of Iowa* 1882
Γ   *Iowa State University* 1913
Δ   *Drake University* 1961

KANSAS
A   *University of Kansas* 1882
B   *Washburn University* 1910
Γ   *Kansas State University* 1920
Δ   *Wichita State University* 1959
E   *Emporia State University* 1968
Z   *Southwestern College* 1995
H   *Kansas State Univ., Salina* 2002

KENTUCKY
AΔ   *Centre College* 1850
E   *University of Kentucky* 1966
H   *Western Kentucky University* 1966
Θ   *Eastern Kentucky University* 1969

MANITOBA
A   *University of Manitoba* 1930

MARYLAND
A   *University of Maryland* 1930
B   *McDaniel College* 1971
Γ   *Washington College* 1992

MASSACHUSETTS
Γ   *Massachusetts Inst. of Tech* 1932

MICHIGAN
A   *University of Michigan Colony*
B   *Michigan State University* 1873
Δ   *Kettering University* 1964
E   *Northwood University* 1983

MINNESOTA
B   *Minnesota State University* 1964

ΦΔΘ The Standard for Brotherhood
Phi Delta Theta International Fraternity

As of July 2004

★ *Chapter*
☆ *Colony*

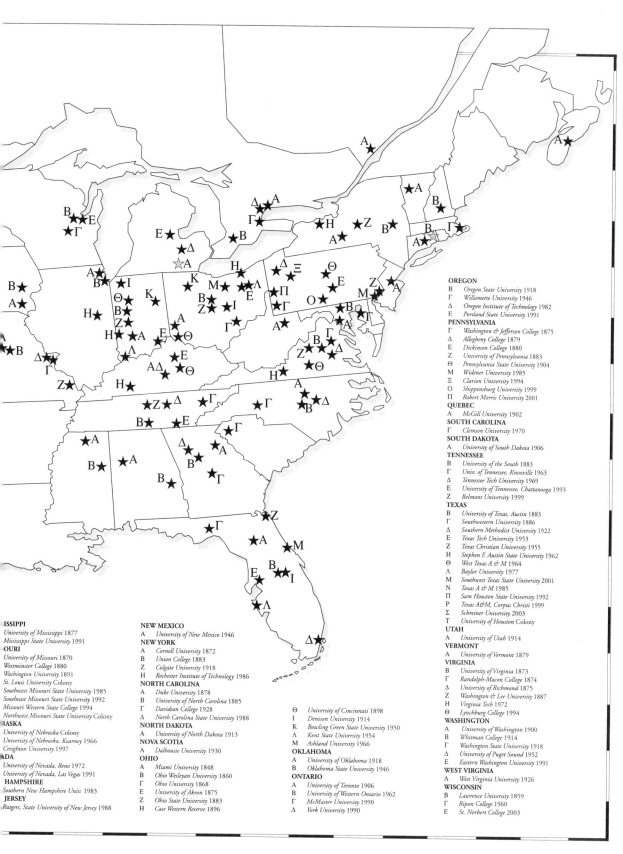

OREGON
B   *Oregon State University* 1918
Γ   *Willamette University* 1946
Δ   *Oregon Institute of Technology* 1982
E   *Portland State University* 1991

PENNSYLVANIA
Γ   *Washington & Jefferson College* 1875
Δ   *Allegheny College* 1879
E   *Dickinson College* 1880
Z   *University of Pennsylvania* 1883
Θ   *Pennsylvania State University* 1904
M   *Widener University* 1985
Ξ   *Clarion University* 1994
O   *Shippensburg University* 1999
Π   *Robert Morris University* 2001

QUEBEC
A   *McGill University* 1902

SOUTH CAROLINA
Γ   *Clemson University* 1970

SOUTH DAKOTA
A   *University of South Dakota* 1906

TENNESSEE
B   *University of the South* 1883
Γ   *Univ. of Tennessee, Knoxville* 1963
Δ   *Tennessee Tech University* 1969
E   *University of Tennessee, Chattanooga* 1993
Z   *Belmont University* 1999

TEXAS
B   *University of Texas, Austin* 1883
Γ   *Southwestern University* 1886
Δ   *Southern Methodist University* 1922
E   *Texas Tech University* 1953
Z   *Texas Christian University* 1955
H   *Stephen F. Austin State University* 1962
Θ   *West Texas A & M* 1964
Λ   *Baylor University* 1977
M   *Southwest Texas State University* 2001
N   *Texas A & M* 1985
Π   *Sam Houston State University* 1992
P   *Texas A&M, Corpus Christi* 1999
Σ   *Schreiner University* 2003
T   *University of Houston* Colony

UTAH
A   *University of Utah* 1914

VERMONT
A   *University of Vermont* 1879

VIRGINIA
B   *University of Virginia* 1873
Γ   *Randolph-Macon College* 1874
Δ   *University of Richmond* 1875
Z   *Washington & Lee University* 1887
H   *Virginia Tech* 1972
Θ   *Lynchburg College* 1994

WASHINGTON
A   *University of Washington* 1900
B   *Whitman College* 1914
Γ   *Washington State University* 1918
Δ   *University of Puget Sound* 1952
E   *Eastern Washington University* 1991

WEST VIRGINIA
A   *West Virginia University* 1926

WISCONSIN
B   *Lawrence University* 1859
Γ   *Ripon College* 1960
E   *St. Norbert College* 2003

ISSIPPI
University of Mississippi 1877
Mississippi State University 1991

OURI
University of Missouri 1870
Westminster College 1880
Washington University 1891
St. Louis University Colony
Southwest Missouri State University 1985
Southeast Missouri State University 1992
Missouri Western State College 1994
Northwest Missouri State University Colony

RASKA
University of Nebraska Colony
University of Nebraska, Kearney 1966
Creighton University 1997

ADA
University of Nevada, Reno 1972
University of Nevada, Las Vegas 1991

HAMPSHIRE
Southern New Hampshire Univ. 1983

JERSEY
Rutgers, State University of New Jersey 1988

NEW MEXICO
A   *University of New Mexico* 1946

NEW YORK
A   *Cornell University* 1872
B   *Union College* 1883
Z   *Colgate University* 1918
H   *Rochester Institute of Technology* 1986

NORTH CAROLINA
A   *Duke University* 1878
B   *University of North Carolina* 1885
Γ   *Davidson College* 1928
Δ   *North Carolina State University* 1988

NORTH DAKOTA
A   *University of North Dakota* 1913

NOVA SCOTIA
A   *Dalhousie University* 1930

OHIO
A   *Miami University* 1848
B   *Ohio Wesleyan University* 1860
E   *Ohio University* 1868
E   *University of Akron* 1875
Z   *Ohio State University* 1883
H   *Case Western Reserve* 1896

Θ   *University of Cincinnati* 1898
I   *Denison University* 1914
K   *Bowling Green State University* 1950
Λ   *Kent State University* 1954
M   *Ashland University* 1966

OKLAHOMA
A   *University of Oklahoma* 1918
B   *Oklahoma State University* 1946

ONTARIO
A   *University of Toronto* 1906
B   *University of Western Ontario* 1962
Γ   *McMaster University* 1990
Δ   *York University* 1990

B. Palmer fund is more than $4 million.

The David D. Banta Endowment Fund: The establishment of an endowment fund designed to support the David D. Banta Memorial Library located in the General Headquarters Building became a reality through the generosity and personal direction of George Banta, Jr., *Wabash '14,* past president of the General Council. The fund was officially established in December of 1955.

Income from the fund is used for the operation and maintenance of the Library dedicated to the memory of David D. Banta, *Indiana 1855,* one of the first 75 men initiated into the Fraternity and the first of five generations of Banta Phis. This fund was merged with the Phi Delta Theta Educational Foundation in 1984.

Alumni Organizations

As there exists a significant volunteer and staff structure to oversee the operations of the International Fraternity, so too exists a group of alumni organized to oversee operations of the Fraternity's interests on a local level. These local alumni organize to maintain chapter houses and keep the brotherhood alive well beyond the undergraduate years.

Alumni clubs: Alumni clubs are associations with the purpose of fostering loyalty to the Fraternity among members who are no longer in college. They are established by the authority of the General Council in localities where a sufficient number of alumni members reside, upon submission of a petition signed by not less than ten members. Every alumni club which has conducted regularly scheduled meetings during the college year preceding a General Convention, and which has been officially recognized by the General Council, may elect a delegate to the General Convention who may be entitled to vote.

House corporations: The house corporation of a chapter is made up of dedicated Phis who are elected as volunteer trustees of a nonprofit corporation formed to own and operate a chapter house for a Phi Delta Theta chapter. The house corporation is organized and incorporated under the laws of the respective state or province and serves as the legal entity which holds title to any property owned. The house corporation board of directors, which includes at least two undergraduate members, acts as the landlord of the chapter house. It also holds responsibility for the upkeep and maintenance of the chapter house, payment of mortgages and property taxes, and the building of a reserve fund to insulate the corporation from future financial hardship. The house corporation is the entity to which the Walter B. Palmer Foundation can make loans for the renovation or building of a chapter facility.

General Headquarters

The General Headquarters of the Fraternity is located in Oxford, Ohio, and is under the direction of the Executive Vice President. He acts as secretary to the General Council, prepares and distributes supplies among the chapters and officers of the Fraternity, collects all dues and special assessments, keeps account of all receipts and disbursements, visits active chapters and alumni clubs and acts as business manager of the Fraternity publications, and performs such other duties as the General Council may direct.

The Headquarters staff is charged with the day-to-day administration and affairs of the Fraternity. These staff members serve as the liaison officers between the General Fraternity and the chapters, to which they make as frequent visits as possible. Many of these visits are made by leadership consultants of the Fraternity.

Leadership consultants are employed by the General Fraternity to counsel the undergraduate members and officers in chapters across North America. The position is held by a young Phi who is a recent college graduate.

Typically, the consultant travels from chapter to chapter throughout the academic year. He spends from two to six days at each location, where he attends chapter, Phikeia, and committee meetings, counsels with individual chapter officers, meets with the chapter adviser, a university representative, and a member of the house corporation, and, when possible, attends a meeting of the local alumni club.

The term Leadership Consultant is a latecomer to the Fraternity. The first traveling member of the staff was actually the first executive secretary who was employed in 1923. The 1925 Convention authorized the employment of an assistant secretary, or as the post became popularly known, traveling secretary. The term field secretary became standard nomenclature in 1956. The title was changed to chapter consultant in 1971 to better describe the duty and function inherent in the position and changed to Leadership Consultant in 1997 to reflect further advances in the position.

The director of risk management position was created in 1995 to administer the insurance, housing and risk management program. This person oversees the insurance needs of the Fraternity, sits on the Housing Commission, and works in conjunction with the Palmer Foundation.

The director of chapter services oversees the leadership consultants and manages the chapter-related matters of General Headquarters. He is often the first contact undergraduates have with General Headquarters, and as such he consults with them on a variety of matters from risk management and officer programming to ritual and Phikeia education.

The position of director of communications was created in 1991 when the General Council decided that a permanent staff position was needed to oversee the editing of The Scroll and other publications, as well as to organize the public relations. Previously, the editor of the Fraternity magazine had been a volunteer position.

The General Headquarters is also the location of the Educational Foundation staff, which consists of three full-time staff members.

General Headquarters is the vital, active center where the business of the Fraternity is transacted. However, it is more than that; through its constant contact with the undergraduate members and alumni, it keeps fresh and current those intangible, spiritual values

"Chief Executives"

Arthur R. Priest
DePauw 1891
Executive   Secretary,
1923–37.

Paul C. Beam
Indiana-Illinois '25
Executive   Secretary,
1937–55.

Robert J. Miller
New Mexico '50
Executive   Vice
President,† 1955–91

Robert A. Biggs
Georgia Southern '76
Executive   Vice
President, 1991–
present

† The title of the chief executive changed in 1971
to Executive Vice President.

that are the heart of Phi Delta Theta.

Laws of the Fraternity

The supreme governing document of the Fraternity is The Bond of Phi Delta Theta, the original document drafted by Robert Morrison and John McMillan Wilson at the Fraternity's founding. Every Phi must sign The Bond upon initiation, and every initiate is bound by its precepts. The Bond is unalterable, and violation of its cannons is grounds for expulsion from the Fraternity.

Although no laws of the Fraternity may be passed that violate the integrity of The Bond, the General Convention has the power to create laws to govern the administration and organization of the Fraternity. The laws that make up the Constitution and General Statutes of Phi Delta Theta are called The Code.

Chapters, alumni clubs, general officers, and even General Council members are bound by the laws of the Fraternity that make up The Code. The Code addresses procedure for expansion of the Fraternity, discipline of members and chapters, election of the General Council, membership, and the descriptions of the general officer positions. A complete copy of The Code is provided at the back of this manual and should be read by all members of the Fraternity.

Initiated members may be expelled for financial reasons, conduct unworthy of a Phi, or violations of The Bond or The Code only after a two-thirds vote of the chapter or a four-fifths vote of the General Council. Initiates may resign from membership only after a four-fifths vote of approval from the General Council.

Chapters may be disciplined by the General Council or Province President with probationary measures or escrow, which is a temporary suspension of the charter until certain terms are met. Only the General Council may suspend a charter, which may result in the closure of chapter facilities and suspension or expulsion of members. The Fraternity may reorganize sus-pended chapters with new members and reinstate the charter when the new organization becomes able to sustain and govern itself.

Only an act of the General Convention may revoke a charter. A three-fourths vote is required to do so. If the chapter is reestablished, the new founders are listed on the charter, and the issued Bond numbers continue on from the last previously assigned Bond number.

Changes to the Constitution may only be made by a three-fourths vote of two consecutive General Conventions. Changes to the General Statutes may be made only with a three-fourths vote at a single Convention.

Admission of New Chapters

When a group of students at a college or university petitions for establishment of a Phi Delta Theta chapter, the matter is referred to the Survey Commission, a standing committee of not fewer than three members which includes a past president of the General Council and the Executive Vice President who serves as an ex officio member. The Survey Commission conducts a careful examination of the institution to determine, first, whether the welfare of the Fraternity would be served by a chapter so located and, second, whether the petitioning group would be likely to represent Phi Delta Theta creditably.

An institution may also be approved for the establishment of a colony by the unanimous vote of the members of the General Council, the unanimous vote of the members of the Survey Commission, and with the approval of the Province President in whose province the institution is located. This action enables the Fraternity to proceed with the development of a colony with the purpose of eventual chartering. If a local fraternity is already in existence, arrangements may be made to declare it a colony. Otherwise, students, working with local alumni and General Headquarters staff, endeavor to establish an interest group which may then become a colony. After the colony satisfies the standards of operation established by the General Council, a charter will be granted upon approval by three-fourths of the chapters in the province in which the institution is located and the approval of the president of the province and the General Council.

Through substantial and well-planned growth, the Fraternity extends today over the wide reaches of the United States and Canada.

Questions

1. How was the Fraternity governed before 1880?
2. What changes occurred at the Convention of 1880?
3. What are the powers of the Convention? Who can vote at the Convention?
4. What are the powers and responsibilities of the General Council? How are they elected?
5. Who are the current members of the General Council?
6. What powers are reserved to the local chapter?
7. What is the function of the chapter adviser?
8. Where is the General Headquarters located? What are its functions?
9. Who is the current executive vice president? What are his duties?
10. What is the Phi Delta Theta Foundation?
11. What is the Frank J. R. Mitchell Fund?
12. What is the Walter B. Palmer Fund?
13. What is an alumni club?

Essays

1. Describe the process by which a group obtains a charter.
2. What is the value and significance of belonging to an international brotherhood?

VI

"You must guard against elation. Do not look at the past as a thing that should be satisfying; look at it only as something in general that was well done. Thank God for it, but go and do something better."
ROBERT MORRISON, MIAMI 1849

The Chapter

MANY CHAPTERS COMPRISE the realm of Phi Delta Theta. Each is a semi-autonomous unit of the entire General Fraternity, one part of the whole. Yet each chapter has its own character, its own traditions, and its own sense of purpose. Thus, it would seem that the chapters are very diverse, and to a certain extent they are. Each individual unit, however, has the same primary purpose: to bring the Phi Delta Theta experience to each respective campus.

That purpose of the Fraternity is to promote the high principles which constituted the foundation of the organization, declared in The Bond of Phi Delta Theta. These principles, so eloquently penned by Robert Morrison and John McMillan Wilson, predicate an organized brotherhood in which members support each other in daily life.

Indeed, the Six Founders of Phi Delta Theta were visionaries. Through The Bond,

Facing Page: Phis gather at the Phi Delta Theta Gates at Miami University during the 1993 Leadership College. The Gates were a gift from the Fraternity to Miami in 1973.

they outlined ideals practical both to the individual and to the chapter. They can be applied in a variety of areas of chapter life. With these ideals in mind, it is easier to further define exactly what a chapter is.

The chapter, first and foremost, is a family. Like a family, the brothers participate in activities allowing them to work, live, and socialize together. It is an environment conducive to the development of long-lasting ties, the sharing of similar aspirations, and the fostering of concern for others.

In another frame, the chapter is also a classroom. In this setting, members learn a great deal including management ideas, event-planning strategies, important social skills, and perspectives on topics of interest on all college campuses. A college education is not merely learning from textbooks or lectures, and the Fraternity provides this important education outside the standard curriculum.

The chapter is also a democracy. Group decision making and management are part of the fraternity experience. Brothers participate in the election of chapter leaders and vote on the various policies and activities of the organization. By working together in a democratic society, members learn valuable organization and leadership skills.

The Phi Delta Theta chapter is also a business. The members develop and approve budgets, receive and disperse money, procure various services and products, and follow general accounting practices with monthly and annual financial statements. Through this process, the brothers and Phikeias learn the importance of sound fiscal planning and financial management.

In the final analysis, the chapter is an opportunity. It provides the chance for members to grow and develop as leaders, helps build lifelong friendships, encourages good scholarship performance, and teaches the individual responsibility to a larger group.

Activities of the Chapter

The undergraduate chapter is involved in numerous activities which are educational to the members, essential to the chapter's existence, and exciting for the participants. Although each individual chapter adds its own style and enthusiasm to these activities, every chapter participates in them. Listed below are a few of these activities.

Membership recruitment. The process by which the fraternity chapter acquires new members is commonly known as "recruitment" (preferred) or "rush." There is a constant need to identify prospective members in order to continue the existence and function of the chapter. Every member must do his part to help in this vitally important process. Together the members of the chapter set goals regarding the size of the incoming Phikeia class and the type of men that should be recruited. Most chapters also require

THE CHAPTER HOUSE AT THE UNIVERSITY OF MISSOURI.

a vote of the entire membership to determine who may receive an invitation to join the chapter.

Successful membership recruitment requires the involvement of each individual of the chapter. Although recruitment activities are often planned by the recruitment chairman and his committee, each brother must become involved in the process. Membership recruitment is a time to make new acquaintances and friends and through this process, to determine who will be a part of the brotherhood. It is a time when every member has direct input regarding the future of the chapter. It is certainly a time when an individual's zeal for the chapter is most noticeably on display.

Phikeia Education

A positive Phikeia education program seeks to assimilate new members into the chapter, placing emphasis on the individual and avoiding traditional rites-of-passage activities. The chapter attempts to create a program whereby concepts such as pride, acceptance, understanding, self-respect, and confidence motivate the Phikeias to succeed. This is perhaps one of the most important processes in the chapter.

As in the recruitment process, responsibility for the success of the Phikeia education program falls upon each member of the chapter. Brothers are expected to set a good example for Phikeias to follow and participate in some of the activities involving the Phikeia class. Phikeias should be drawn into the activities of the entire chapter through encouragement by the brothers to participate in athletics, in the social life of the chapter, and in the committee system as well as the other programs of the Fraternity. The Phikeias are expected to learn about the operations, history, and ideals of Phi Delta Theta during the

THE CHAPTER HOUSE AT SOUTHERN METHODIST UNIVERSITY.

tory, and ideals of Phi Delta Theta during the Phikeia education program.

Scholarship

Because sound learning is one of the three cardinal principles of Phi Delta Theta, scholarship is encouraged and emphasized in each chapter of the Fraternity. Education is the primary reason students are enrolled in college, and the chapter must help its members in their efforts to improve their scholastic performance.

Most chapters have a scholarship program that assists the members and Phikeias with the rigors of the college curriculum. This program generally consists of minimum grade point requirements for the good standing of the members, study hall, quiet hours in the chapter house, awards and incentives for scholastic achievement, test files, and a tutor system. A chapter house may also provide a library or study room for the members. The end result is a an environment which is conducive to scholastic excellence.

Alumni Relations

Membership in Phi Delta Theta extends well beyond the years in college. Consequently, each chapter develops an alumni relations program as a means to maintain the interests and involvement of its alumni. The Fraternity understands that behind every great chapter are great alumni. It is in the chapter's best interest to cultivate the support and enthusiasm of its alumni.

The chapter's alumni relations program develops the relationship between alumni and the undergraduate chapter. Chapters publish quarterly newsletters describing the chapter's affairs, alumni news, and upcoming alumni events. University homecomings, Founders Day celebrations, and Golden and Silver Le-

THE CHAPTER HOUSE AT THE UNIVERSITY OF MISSISSIPPI.

gion ceremonies are annual events that chapters plan to encourage alumni to return to the university and to build a positive relationship with the alumni.

Community Service

Each chapter of the Fraternity conducts a program of community service and philanthropy. By engaging in activities that help the community, the chapter promotes not only itself, but the General Fraternity as well. Chapters organize a variety of events that help community service organizations or raise money for community charities. Every year the General Fraternity organizes a Community Service Month in April when all the chapters of Phi Delta Theta participate in the service project of their choice.

A good program of community service requires the involvement of all of the members of the chapter. Much effort goes into planning and publicizing events, spending numerous hours on a community service project, and generating funds for a philanthropic event. When the project is complete, members experience a rewarding feeling and a sense of accomplishment that comes only from helping others.

Ritual

The performance of the Phi Delta Theta ritual at weekly chapter meetings serves to reaffirm each individual member's commitment to the vows taken at the time of initiation. The ritual aids in the development of integrity and strong moral character in the members. It teaches the true meaning of the Fraternity and maintains a common bond between every brother in the International Fraternity. The weekly practice of the ritual is one thing every member has in common.

The ritual of Phi Delta Theta is something in which each member takes great pride. It reinforces each member's understanding of the ideals of the Fraternity and generates an enthusiasm within the brotherhood. The careful and thoughtful practice of the ritual by the brothers helps ensure the honor of the Phi Delta Theta membership.

Chapter Organization

Every group or organization needs an internal management structure in order to exist with any sense of order or efficiency. This was true for the first Phi Delta Theta chapter at Miami University. Indeed, during the very first meeting on December 26, 1848, temporary officers and a committee were established. The committee was to report on the adoption of an appropriate motto, bond, and constitution. A meeting on December 28 was held to further discuss these items. Finally on December 30, 1848, the Immortal Six adopted and accepted the motto created by Robert Morrison, The Bond which was written by Morrison and John McMillan Wilson, and the Constitution. The meeting also served to formally elect officers. Wilson was elected president, Robert Thompson Drake was elected secretary, and Morrison was elected warden. A committee was appointed to prepare bylaws for the group.

From the very beginning of the Fraternity, the Founders used a basic organizational structure within the chapter which included bylaws, officers, committees, and regular chapter meetings. Over the years, many things have changed in the Fraternity, but the concept of meetings, officers, committees, and bylaws as the foundation of chapter organization has remained constant and exists in each chapter today.

Bylaws

Each chapter of the Fraternity adopts its own bylaws. This is usually the first item of business as a new chapter is being formed. Just as the Constitution and General Statutes serve to define and direct the actions of the General Fraternity, a chapter's bylaws outline the policies and regulations of the respective chapter. It should be noted that nothing in a chapter's bylaws can supersede the provisions of The Bond or the Constitution and General Statutes of Phi Delta Theta.

Typically, chapter bylaws are very similar. The bylaws begin with the chapter constitution, outlining a statement of policy of the chapter, stating the mission of the chapter, and declaring the purpose of the bylaws and how they may be amended. These policies should also consist of a declaration by the chapter to support the International Fraternity's position on hazing and policies on risk management.

Other areas addressed in the bylaws include powers and policies of chapter meetings, the officer election process, duties of officers, the chapter committee structure, membership selection process, financial responsibilities, and the chapter's judicial mechanism. Additional topics such as house rules, initiation requirements, and commissary programs may be covered at the discretion of each chapter.

The bylaws serve as an organizational guide. They should be detailed and specific. They should outline the chapter's rules and processes. Therefore, it is important that the bylaws be followed by the chapter. They are an important part of the democratic process of the organization, likened to a country's national constitution. It is highly recommended each brother and Phikeia receive a copy of the bylaws so he may become familiar with them and abide by their provisions.

Officers of the Chapter

The roster of chapter officers has increased significantly since the first officer election on

THE CHAPTER HOUSE AT WICHITA STATE UNIVERSITY.

December 30, 1848, at Ohio Alpha. The General Statutes of Phi Delta Theta currently provide for 15 chapter officers. However, there are usually between 15 and 20 officers or chairmen that most chapters elect within their organizations. These officers are listed below with a brief description summarizing their duties.

President. The president oversees all aspects of the chapter. He presides over chapter meetings, sits on the Executive Committee, and serves as the chapter's spokesman. He is the chapter's liaison with the chapter advisory board chairman, province president, General Headquarters, alumni, campus administration, the Interfraternity Council, and other fraternities and sororities. He is generally responsible for seeing that the chapter operates smoothly.

Vice President. The vice president assumes the president's responsibilities in his absence. Additionally, he serves as the chairman of the chapter's Executive Committee, and as such, is responsible for coordinating the activities of all chapter officers and committees. He is often in charge of the daily internal activities of the chapter. He is also charged with the responsibility of seeing that all proper reports are submitted to the General Headquarters.

Treasurer. The treasurer has the charge of collecting all dues and fees from the members, dispersing expenditures within the chapter's approved budget, and keeping a proper record of all financial affairs of the chapter. He prepares and submits a monthly financial report to the chapter, province president, and the General Headquarters. The treasurer serves on the Executive Committee.

Secretary. The secretary is responsible for keeping chapter meeting minutes and roll. He sees that the bylaws are accurate and modified if the chapter changes them in any way. He conducts the official correspondence of the chapter, also serving as the chapter's liaison to

The Scroll. He maintains the chapter roster and membership files. He is a member of the Executive Committee.

Phikeia Educator. The phikeia educator is responsible for the supervision of Phikeia activities, including the planning and implementation of a sound program of new member education which provides opportunities for leadership development, promotes the ideals of the Fraternity, and sets a base for fraternal living beyond initiation. He helps the Phikeias make the smooth transition to full membership, teaching them Fraternity lore, chapter operations, scholarship, and brotherhood, with the aid of the Phikeia Education Committee and the other chapter officers. He often sits on the Executive Committee.

Alumni Secretary. The alumni secretary works to maintain a good relationship between the chapter and its alumni through an alumni relations program. The program usually consists of publishing an alumni newsletter and planning and promoting alumni events such as Founders Day and homecoming. He maintains a record of alumni members and often works with local alumni clubs.

Recruitment Chairman. The recruitment chairman heads the Recruitment Committee of the chapter. It is this committee's duty to develop a membership recruitment program which encourages the chapter to pursue new candidates for membership. As recruiting new members is vital to the future of the chapter, the rush chairman is a very important position. The rush chairman and his committee coordinate all formal and informal recruitment events, and they conduct workshops and retreats to teach members proper recruitment techniques.

Scholarship Chairman. This individual chairs the Scholarship Committee of the chapter. The committee develops and implements a program which promotes the principle of sound learning, among both the brothers and Phikeias. The chairman strives to provide educational opportunities to the brothers through the resources available at the college or university. The program can include study tables, speakers on time management, study partners, and awards for members who achieve scholastic excellence.

Historian. This officer maintains a historical record of the chapter's activities during his term. He uses photo albums, scrapbooks, and an annual written history to record the events of the chapter. He is also responsible for submitting to the General Headquarters reports dealing with Phikeia class membership, initiations, and Bond numbers.

House Manager. The house manager oversees a property management program that focuses on house maintenance, obeys health and fire regulations, and creates a clean and safe living environment for the members. He

organizes the members in weekly house cleaning and property maintenance projects, and he usually works closely with the house corporation to coordinate house improvement projects and major house renovations.

Steward. In those chapters with a commissary program, the steward serves as the kitchen manager. He works closely with the cook on the planning of menus for chapter meals. He also oversees the cleanliness of the kitchen facility, thus insuring proper health regulations are met. He is the liaison between the treasurer, the cook, and the chapter. He organizes chapter crews to clean the kitchen facilities.

Warden. This important position serves as the chapter ritualist. It is the warden's job to oversee the education of the brothers in the teachings of The Bond and ritual of Phi Delta Theta. He coordinates the initiation ceremony with the president. He also serves

THE CHAPTER HOUSE AT MIAMI UNIVERSITY.

to maintain order and proper meeting decorum at weekly chapter meetings.

Community Service Chairman. This chairman and his committee direct the community service and philanthropic activities of the chapter through a program promoting positive interaction between the Fraternity and the local and campus communities.

Social Chairman. The social chairman, with his committee, coordinates and organizes the social functions of the chapter. He works directly with other fraternity and sorority social chairmen to plan joint events. The social chairman is responsible for insuring the chapter's social program is structured on an awareness of risk management while maintaining a fun, yet tasteful, social event. He may also be responsible for any alcohol awareness or risk management education within the chapter.

Chaplain. The chaplain conducts all religious exercises of the chapter. He also seeks to develop integrity and strong moral character in the members. He often coordinates brotherhood events, acts as a counselor, and organizes events or ideas that promote the chapter's morale.

Fund-Raising Chairman. Often the income generated solely from the members' dues is insufficient to run the daily operations of the chapter. Therefore, the fund-raising chairman heads a committee charged with organizing ways for the chapter to raise additional money.

Chorister. It is the job of the chorister to teach the chapter the songs of the Fraternity. He organizes serenades for sororities, and he prepares the chapter for any singing competitions. He leads the Fraternity in song during chapter meetings, before meals, or at other appropriate events.

Foundation Representative. The foundation representative promotes the Phi Delta Theta Foundation scholarships to the chapter, coordinating the chapter's nomination of a member to be considered for one of these awards. He also assists the brother in the formal application process and assists the scholarship chairman.

Awards Chairman. This officer oversees the chapter's applications for individual and chapter awards given annually by the General Fraternity. He prepares the awards reports to be sent to the Awards Committee at the General Headquarters. He is almost always assisted by the executive officers in this endeavor.

Librarian. It is the duty of the librarian to develop and maintain a chapter library consisting of items pertinent to the Fraternity. Such items would include past copies of THE SCROLL, The History of Phi Delta Theta, chapter histories, and academic reference material as well as other items of interest to the chapter. The librarian may also act as a caretaker of the chapter's trophies and composite photographs.

Other Officers. Each chapter may have other elected or appointed offices. The names and scope of these positions are quite varied. Often they include offices such as IFC representative, intramural chairman, homecoming coordinator, etc. Consult your chapter's by-laws to see if any other positions exist.

Committees of the Chapter

The committee system is vitally important in the structure of the chapter. Committees execute the initiatives and programs of the chapter, and therefore a large part of the chapter's planning and activities are accomplished through committee work. In addition to the work they accomplish, committees help to involve members in the chapter organization who do not serve as officers or chairmen.

Each chapter has numerous committees. The functions, responsibilities, and members of the committees are dictated by the needs of the chapter. The three main types of committees include: the Executive Committee, standing committees and special committees.

As the administrative arm of the chapter, the Executive Committee is the driving force of the Fraternity. It is responsible for organizing and motivating the chapter membership. As the unified leadership body of the chapter, the Executive Committee establishes programs and priorities to accomplish the goals set by the chapter. The ultimate success of the chapter lies with the Executive Committee's knowledge of the strengths and weaknesses of the chapter and its ability to establish initiatives which address these areas.

The Executive Committee meets each week to prepare an agenda for the chapter meeting and to discuss other important issues facing the chapter. The committee's procedure usually includes reports of officers, formulation of the chapter meeting agenda, establishment of objectives, evaluation of chapter goals, and motivation of the chapter membership.

The vice president is the chairman of the Executive Committee. The president, treasurer, and usually the secretary are also members. Other officers or chairmen that sit on the Executive Committee are determined by the chapter's bylaws.

Standing committees

Standing committees are responsible for developing and maintaining the specific programs of the chapter. These committees are determined by the chapter's bylaws, but usually include committees on membership recruitment, membership education, finances, alumni relations, community service, judicial board, and scholarship. These committees establish the goals of the respective programs, implement the plans, prepare for events, and

THE CHAPTER HOUSE AT PURDUE UNIVERSITY.

evaluate the programs' success. Some standing committees are discussed below.

Finance Committee. The Finance Committee is responsible for developing and maintaining a sound fiscal policy for the chapter. Its specific duties include developing a budget for chapter approval, insuring that the budget is followed, and assisting the treasurer in the collection of accounts receivable.

Scholarship Committee. It is the duty of this committee to supervise programs that promote the scholarship of the entire chapter. The committee develops the chapter's scholarship program, assists the scholarship chairman with monitoring members' scholastic performance, implements a system of scholarship awards, and supervises study halls.

Phikeia Education Committee. The Phikeia Education Committee creates and institutes a positive Phikeia education program. Its goal is to execute the education program and to monitor the progress of the Phikeias. The committee also reviews the performance of the Phikeias and may act as a disciplinarian for cases involving the Phikeias in the form of a Pallas Committee.

Recruitment Committee. The Recruitment Committee oversees the membership recruitment program of the chapter. It assesses the chapter's need for additional members and then plans strategies to recruit them. The committee plans recruitment events, motivates the chapter, and educates the members about recruitment.

Risk Management Committee. The Risk Management Committee assists in the education of the chapter on risk management issues in all areas of operation.

Other standing committees may include an Alumni Relations Committee which coordinates all alumni activities of the chapter; a Community Service Committee which orga-

THE CHAPTER HOUSE AT UNIVERSITY OF TORONTO.

nizes community service and philanthropic events; a Social Committee which plans the social program of the chapter; a Public Relations Committee which attempts to promote the chapter's image, and an Awards Committee which prepares the chapter's applications for campus or General Fraternity awards.

Special Committees

In many instances, the chapter may appoint a special committee to plan or administer a special activity or program. Such a committee is usually dissolved upon the completion of its assigned task. Some special committees would be: Bylaw Review Committee, Greek Week Committee, Homecoming Committee, Parents Weekend Committee, Founders Day Committee, etc.

The Chapter Meeting

The chapter meeting provides a setting for an important part of the Fraternity experience. It is through this weekly gathering of the brothers that issues are discussed, legislation is proposed, and plans are approved. The chapter meeting serves as a forum for all the members to exchange comments, ideas, suggestions, and complaints. This weekly gathering also allows the members to enjoy the company of the brothers and to share personal news about each other.

The meeting is chaired by the president. Items on the agenda include reports of officers and committees, general business, and roll call. The election of officers, proposals for new members, and modifications to the bylaws are all held during chapter meetings.

Each weekly meeting of a Phi Delta Theta chapter has opening and closing ritualistic ceremonies. Through these ceremonies, the principles of the Fraternity are reaffirmed by the brothers. For this reason, all chapter meet-

THE CHAPTER HOUSE AT UNIVERSITY OF SOUTH DAKOTA.

ings are secret, and only initiated members may be in attendance.

Parliamentary Procedure

Parliamentary procedure is the machinery of a democracy through which the voice of the public achieves expression. It is also the means by which a democracy's self-molded system and control are created and perfected. In a fraternity chapter meeting, parliamentary procedure functions to give every member his proper chance to express his views, keep meetings moving smoothly, prevent long-winded dissertations, discourage hot tempers, and generally to get chapter business performed efficiently and effectively. It has the value for the individual of giving him practice in the arts of impromptu speaking and diplomatic appeal, considering the viewpoint of others and adjusting his policies in minor particulars to gain a major end, that fairness may be done to all and chapter progress expedited.

Probably the best-known and most widely used manual of parliamentary procedure is ROBERT'S RULES OF ORDER.

Parliamentary law is simple in principle and easy to practice. If one knows the vocabulary, the rules are twice as easy. It is for this reason that a glossary is given first. This glossary of terms will make it much easier for you to become familiar with general meeting procedure. The Phikeias should practice using these rules in their own meetings to prepare them for the responsibilities of an initiated member participating in a chapter meeting.

Amend. To change a motion either by adding to it, taking from it, or altering it.

Business, Order of. The regular program of procedure.

Commit. To refer to a committee.

Chair. The chairman or presiding officer.

Debate. Discussion over a motion.

THE CHAPTER HOUSE AT BUTLER UNIVERSITY.

Division. A vote whereby all who are in favor and all who are opposed to a motion stand separately in groups as the chairman calls for the "ayes" and "nays."

Floor. The privilege of speaking before the assembly. When one "obtains the floor," he has an opportunity to speak.

Motion. A formal proposal to a meeting that it take certain action. It is a "motion" when stated by its proponent and until repeated by the chairman for acceptance or rejection after debate, at which time it becomes a "question."

Order of the Day. Regular order or program of business.

Question. The "question" in parliamentary law is a proposition or motion after discussion and after it has been placed before the meeting for action by the chairman. To "move the previous question" is to demand that the chairman take a vote on a motion which is being discussed. A question, when adopted, becomes an order, resolution, or vote.

Refer. To refer to a committee.

Resolution. The act of an assembly the purpose of which is to express opinions or purposes, and not to command.

Rules, Suspension of. When the assembly wishes to do something that cannot be done without violating its own rules, and yet it is not in conflict with its constitution, or bylaws, or with the fundamental principles of parliamentary law, it suspends the rules that interfere with the proposed action.

Second. A motion, in order to be considered by the meeting, must have a "second," a sponsor in the form of a second member who indicates that he will support the motion by saying, "I second the motion."

Table. The "table" in parliamentary law is literally that speaker's table, but to "lay on the table" or "to table" a motion means to delay action on it.

Rules of Procedure

There are hundreds of rules of parliamentary law. Many are so involved and technical as to be seldom used. All rules are to be found scattered through the leading parliamentary manuals, but for convenience the following more common and fundamental ones are included here.

Duties of a member.
- To remain quiet and seated.
- To obtain the floor from the Chair.
- To refrain from insults or threats.
- To keep to the question at hand.
- To avoid personal argument.
- To vote on all questions.

Rights of a member.
- To express freely his opinions, but not to speak a second time on a question if someone who has not yet spoken desires the floor.
- To ask a speaker a question or correct a misstatement through the Chair.
- To change his vote before the Chair announces the result of the vote.

Powers of the chairman.
- To decide in what order speakers shall be recognized.
- To refuse to recognize absurd or frivolous motions.
- To restrain speakers within the limits of the rules of order.
- To enforce good decorum.
- To appoint committees.
- To decide points of order.
- To vote in cases only where his vote would change the result.
- To make, second, or discuss a motion only when the vice president or next ranking officer is called to preside. If the president speaks on a motion, he may

not resume the chair until the motion is disposed of.
- To speak in order to give information but not to influence debate.

Motions. The regular steps in considering a motion are as follows:

- Presentation, *"I move that . . ."*
- Second. Nominations need no second.
- Stating the motion.
- Discussion.
- Vote.
- Announcing the vote.

Questions

1. Why is membership recruitment important?
2. What is the purpose of Phikeia education?
3. How does scholarship relate to the Fraternity?
4. Why does Phi Delta Theta participate in community service?
5. List the officers in the chapter who sit on the Executive Committee. Who is the chairman?
6. What purpose do bylaws serve? How are bylaws created? How are they changed?
7. List all of the chapter officers and the primary duty of each officer.
8. List possible chapter standing committees and the chairman of each committee within your chapter. What are the duties of each committee?
9. What purpose does parliamentary procedure serve?

Essays

1. What chapter office would you like to hold? Why?
2. What is the importance of ritual in the chapter? Why should it be performed?

VII

"The Fraternity must always work in harmony with the college for the true ends of education."
ARTHUR R. PRIEST, DEPAUW 1891

Scholarship & Sound Learning

BY NOW, YOU HAVE learned that sound learning is one of the three cardinal principles of Phi Delta Theta Fraternity. Scholarship is an important aspect of Fraternity life. The Founders of the Fraternity valued learning and understood its importance in life. The most important point about scholarship is that good performance comes only through the desire to study and to penetrate beyond the surface. A good student maintains an interest in understanding the subject and is committed to doing well.

To become a good student, one must develop a positive attitude toward learning and scholarship. Psychologists know that people learn and retain more if they see meaning in what they study. The meaningfulness of the material will depend on the attitude that one has toward knowledge, and whether the person sees value in being competent and having knowledge of the subject.

As a Phikeia, you have an obligation to perform well scholastically. By making the decision to attend a college or university, you have made a commitment to succeed academically. This commitment is the most important you will make in your college career. If you expect to be an active member of the chapter or be a chapter leader, you must make grades that are creditable.

One of the priorities of the Phikeia education program is to ensure that all Phikeias have the time to study and prepare adequately for their classes. The program will introduce resources on campus that will help you succeed in class. Most people who do well academically are aware of the many resources on campus and know how to use them.

Phi Delta Theta places a great amount of importance on academic achievement. The Educational Foundation offers nearly 50 scholarships to undergraduate members and nearly 20 fellowships to Phi-graduate students each year. The Canadian Scholarship Foundation

---

Facing Page: The Morrison Oak was planted near Elliott Hall at Miami University on March 15, 1899, Brother Morrison's birthday. The white oak sapling was taken from Morrison's home in Fulton, Missouri.

offers scholarship grants to Canadian Phis. In addition, the Graduate Educational Adviser Program assists alumni going to graduate school. This program provides room, board, and a scholarship for a Phi Delta Theta graduate student to act as an academic adviser to a chapter.

The General Fraternity also provides chapters with a regular newsletter that provides academic advice and programs to enhance the chapters' scholarship programs.

If you plan to succeed academically, it is important that you make scholarship your top priority. Remember, the Fraternity should not be a hindrance to academic success, rather, it should enhance and complement it. As a Phikeia, the easiest way to earn good grades is to establish goals, go to class regularly, complete the assigned work, and become acquainted with your instructors.

Time Management

The ability to use one's time effectively can make the difference between an *A* or a *B*. Those students who consistently make the dean's list know how to use their time. How do you use your time? It might surprise you to see how much extra time you really have to study. Using a personal time-analysis chart allows you to evaluate your day. Enter your activities for a typical day on a chart divided into hour blocks for one week. This will determine how you really spend your time and how you can maximize your available time to study. You can often find charts and other time management resources at your campus' Study Resource Center or other student services office.

No one should be without a "To Do List." Many daily planners have them. You can buy planners in most bookstores. Carry it with you so that you can easily remind yourself of your daily schedule and the tasks you must do.

Finally, how do you solve your time management problems? The first step is recognizing that you may have some bad habits that waste time. If you find yourself constantly interrupted by friends, the telephone, other obligations or indecision as to where to start your mound of homework, remember to isolate yourself, limit your access to distractions such as the telephone or television, and divide your homework into smaller tasks. Plan your study sessions, give yourself adequate time, and stick to your plan.

Developing Good Study Habits

Once you have mastered your time schedule, master your scheduled time. Using your study time effectively is even more important than scheduling it.

Find a suitable location for studying. The area should be as distraction-free as possible. Avoid placing things on your desk which may distract you. Do not study close enough to the window to be distracted by outside activity. The room should be well ventilated and have a comfortable temperature. Also, avoid working on a bed or couch; these often prove to be too comfortable.

Use background noise to your advantage. Many students find that while doing involved calculations, soft background noise, like music, can actually help their concentration. This music, however, should be soft enough that you do not find yourself actually thinking about it rather than your work.

Locate suitable areas for group study. When two or more people are studying together, make sure that there is plenty of distraction-free working space for everyone. Empty classrooms are perfect for this type of study. Not only is there plenty of room, but the chalk boards are ideal for problem-solving sessions where one person works at the board while others check his calculations.

Before you begin to study, review your

notes from the last class and skim over the assignments.

When reading new material, always search for unfamiliar words in a dictionary. Underline key points or formulas in your book. If you have a question about something in the assignment, skim a page or go on ahead. If you still have a question, write it down and make a note of the page number so that you can ask your professor during class.

Do not study one subject for more than two or three hours at one sitting. Much more knowledge is retained from the first couple of hours of study than from the third and fourth hours, so change subjects every two or three hours. If it is necessary to study one subject for an extended length of time, take periodic study breaks to relax both your body and your mind.

Always work through any examples in your book to be sure that you understand all of the principles involved. Begin working on each lesson the day that it is assigned. Do not wait until the day before it is due.

Learn to take good notes. Concentrate on everything that the professor says, outlining the key points. Recopy your notes after class in a more organized manner. This will save a lot of study time later, and it will improve your long-term memory of key points.

If you have a question in class, first try to answer it yourself by glancing over recent notes and drawing on personal experiences. If the question is still unanswered, ask your professor. This screening process will lead to more meaningful questions.

Do not be afraid to go to your instructors for help. They are usually eager to help by providing any extra instruction or outside references necessary.

COMFORTABLE & UNDISTRACTING ENVIRONMENT FOR STUDY.
The library or an unused classroom are perfect to review material each day.

Begin studying for examinations several days in advance. Get a good night's sleep before every examination. All-nighters may have saved many students, but they have also hurt just as many.

Anticipate questions that your professors might ask on the test. If you have a copy of an old test, use it for review, but do not look at the questions until you have reviewed all your other material and feel that you are ready for the test. When you are fully prepared, work through the old test as if it were the real test and time yourself so that you can get an idea of how much time to spend answering each question.

Always remember that your education is an investment in your future, so strive to make the most of that investment.

Listening Skills

To be effective in the classroom, a student must develop strong listening skills. Listening is one of the most important skills in learning. The average adult spends about half of his day listening and processing this information. In school, listening ability is as closely related to grade performance as is reading ability. Emotional responses and changes of attitudes result more from listening and comprehending than from reading.

A listening formula, TQLR (tune in, question, listen, review), resembles the reading formula for easy recall and can help you analyze and remember what you hear.

• *Tune in to the speaker.* Be alert, ignore the speaker's mannerisms and try to anticipate the lecture's content from the direction the speaker takes.

ATTENDING CLASSES & TAKING NOTES.
Studies show that consistent attendance greatly improves understanding of the material and grade performance.

• *Question*. What is the lecture about? How does it relate to the text? What are the main points? Ask the lecturer to clarify anything you do not understand.

• *Listen*. Use what the speaker says to organize your notes. Listen for his emphasis, his questions, and his outline. Decide how well he answers your own questions.

• *Review*. As you listen, summarize the main points. Write the main ideas in your own words. Relate what you learn to what you already know. Review your notes regularly to keep your memory fresh.

Note-Taking Skills

Well developed note-taking skills are essential for good performance in the classroom. If a student does not accurately record the material in class, his ability to study successfully is impeded.

A common misconception of note taking is that you will get more from lectures if you don't take notes, but instead reflect on the author's ideas. However, if you don't take notes, you cannot review your reflections later. Another misconception is that you should take notes only on main points, ignoring the details. Main points may not have much meaning later without the details to form a context.

So, the main question is not whether to take notes, but how to take them.

Good notes start with good listening. Develop a mental set by anticipating content on the way to class. Have definite questions in mind about the topic to be discussed and read assignments before class. Pay special attention to introductory remarks and the overview.

Use the TQLR technique throughout the lecture. Try to identify topic sentences and important details. Remember that notes must be complete enough to be able to refresh memory, but they should be short enough to

be easy to read and remember.

Good notes must be orderly. Use an 8½"x 11" notebook, and keep all notes for a single course together in sequence. Remember to date all entries and keep your notes legible.

Use an outline form when taking notes. Indent various levels of details using Roman numerals and capital letters. This may be difficult, but it reveals the lecture's organization and requires you to pay close attention to the lecture.

Arranging your note-taking format will help you reference your notes from the lecture and textbook while leaving room for your own insights and the classroom discussion.

The 2-5-1 format allows two inches in left margin for summary text outline, five inches in the center of the page for lecture notes, and one inch in the right margin for personal remarks, additions or classroom discussion.

Examinations

Before the examination, find out what it will cover. This will give you a "set" for reviewing. No test covers everything taught in a course.

Find out what kind of an examination it will be: objective, essay, or a combination of both. If it is an essay examination, find out whether there will be several short questions of this type or whether there will be one or more long ones, or both. Objective examinations require a specific type of response from you. Essay examinations require something just as specific but different. There are successful techniques to preparing for and taking each kind of test.

Reviewing is a big stumbling block, because the task looks so large that the human tendency is to postpone it. This leads to the all-night cram session which sends you into the examination with a blurred mind filled with a jumble of facts and little sense of proportion.

Start reviewing methodically and early.

Make human nature work for you. Separate review time from work on daily assignments.

Review in short chunks every day, no more than two hours at a time. If you work more than that, your brain tires, and you waste time. If you must work more than that, give yourself a deliberate, unexciting break of 10–15 minutes, before you start again.

Divide the review material in each course into logical sections and concentrate on one at a time. Terminology is a good place to start, if you are weak in it.

Relieve your mind by reviewing your worst subject first. A lot of review is really learning something for the first time, and naturally this will take the most effort.

Review your toughest subject again just before the examination, either the day before or the night before. This is a sensible form of cramming, because it is really review.

There is such a thing as reviewing too early, if you have not studied the material regularly since the course began. Assuming you are average, and there is a lot of material you don't remember, the best time to start is probably about two weeks before a major examination if you are fairly weak in the subject, or a week before it if you are confident in your ability.

Make sure you know certain elementary additional facts about the examination, such as where it is, when it is, and what you are expected and allowed to bring with you. Get there early with the appropriate materials.

During the Examination

Before you start writing, glance over the whole examination. This does two things for you. It gives you an idea of what the examinations covers, where the emphasis lies, and what the main ideas are. Many examinations are composed of a series of short questions all related to one particular aspect of the subject, and a longer question about a different aspect.

Scanning the test relaxes you, because as you glance through it, you will find several questions you feel competent to answer.

Observe the point value of the questions and then figure out a rough time allowance. If the total point value of the test is 100, then a 50-point question is worth about half of your time, regardless of how many questions there are. A quick rule for a one-hour, 100-point test is to divide the point value of each question in half to determine the number of minutes you should spend on it.

Underline all significant words in the directions. Many unfortunate students have penalized themselves, because they did not thoroughly read the directions.

When you begin to work, tackle the questions in the order that appeals to you most. There is nothing sacred about the order in which the questions are asked. Doing well on a question that you feel relatively sure of will be reassuring and will free your mind of tension. The act of writing often unlocks the temporarily blocked mental processes; when you finish that question, you will probably find the others less formidable. On the other hand, you may be the type of person who wants to get the big one off his mind first, and answer the easy one last. If you are writing in an examination book, be sure to identify the questions clearly.

When you are finished, check over your entire paper to see if you have left any questions unanswered, and if you have followed directions.

Don't take time to recopy answers, unless you are sure they are really illegible. You will not be graded on neatness, only on thoroughness and accuracy.

How to Handle Test Anxiety

Examination nerves are common and understandable, and the cure for them is known. You can avoid unproductive nervousness by using certain techniques.

Realize that examination nerves aren't completely bad for you. Do not try to become totally relaxed, because that won't help your performance. Experiments with extremely comfortable seats and limp muscles show that performance under these conditions is poor. Optimal alertness is the key to doing well. The degree of concern and muscular readiness best suited for taking an examination lies somewhere between complete relaxation and too much tension.

Some people flunk themselves. You can avoid it. Past troubles and defeats have built a dismal self-image for some students. They actually make a habit of failing. As a result, after a halfhearted try, they seem to prove they were right! Don't let this happen to you. If you have the failure habit, recognize it and give yourself the chance of success you deserve.

Your energy is best spent on the examination, not on fear. Nervousness can make you concentrate on fear so much that you neglect the examination questions. Remember to think about the work, not the worry. Focus on the questions themselves. You'll be surprised how well this simple redirection of attention works.

You should respect your right answers too. People with exam nerves are often perfectionists, and if they get nine out of ten answers right, they emphasize the one they missed. Credit yourself with what you do right. There is always at least something in that category.

You must, of course, prepare. An absolutely critical rule for avoiding panic and anxiety is preparation for the situations that may cause them. For certain types of exami-

Accomplishing Your Goals.
Studies show a higher percentage of Greeks graduate than non-Greeks.

nations, like the SAT or GRE, almost no preparation is needed or possible, but you can run through the practice tests often available.

You should avoid excessive studying. Staying at your desk or in your study chair may look noble, but it eventually becomes inefficient as you tire. Plan time to rest as well as to study, and indicate these times in your calendar. This relieves you of the anxiety about having enough time. Relaxation and sleep are as important as effective study.

In the Examination Room

During the test expect in the first few minutes to feel nervous. Just wait a few minutes, and this nervous reactions will dissipate. Take two or three deep breaths, let them out slowly.

Next, look over all the questions briefly, to size up what's expected. Answer the easier questions first to accumulate as many points as possible.

Don't spend too much time on any one question, even the hard ones. Many students fail because they answer a few questions beautifully but neglect others that are equally important.

If there is no penalty for wrong answers, then guess. Statistically, this is better than leaving a question blank, and what seems like pure guess work is more often right than wrong. Avoid changing your answers unless you are sure you made an error. Changed answers are more often wrong than right.

If the test is in an essay format, first write down main points on scratch paper without worrying about their sequence. Then, number each point in proper order. Write your essay, following your numbered outline underlining the main points to help the reader follow your thought. Try to write legibly and number your answers plainly.

If you finish early, use the time to check your spelling, punctuation, and grammar.

After the Examination

An excellent way to learn how to take examinations is to analyze what you did after the test is over. When you get your paper back, go over it, noting not only what you did wrong, but why. An hour or two spent in this way may be extremely valuable. See if you detect any avoidable mistakes like misreading directions, wasting time on needless detail, or misreading questions entirely. The next time you have an examination, consciously avoid these problems.

You should also note what you did right! This may save you hours of worry the next time you study for a test. You may have done very well on a question which haunted you for several days. Why did it get such a good reception? Often, such analysis proves genuinely reassuring.

Scholarship and the Campus

Academic success is dependent on understanding the resources available on your campus. Early in your pledge program, you should learn who the key administrators are and what programs and services are offered. These professionals, particularly in the student affairs area, can be helpful in assisting you with study skills.

Some campuses offer study skill centers where you can go for a variety of aids, ranging from help with math to English composition. Check with the specific department to find out specifically what help is available.

You should also develop a working understanding of the library. Most libraries offer instructional tours or short classes on proper use of the library facilities.

Many student affairs programs and services are available on most campuses. Career counseling, financial aid assistance, and personal counseling are most likely offered. Resolving many of these personal issues can help one's mind concentrate in the classroom.

If you do not know where to seek assistance, check with your pledgemaster or the Dean of Students Office.

Avoiding Scholarship Problems
How do you avoid academic problems? If you attend class regularly and are prepared, complete the assignments, and are acquainted with your instructors, chances are much greater that you will succeed. If a student fails to do any of these things, he can easily start to experience low academic performance. Here are some common warning signals:

• Regularly missing class.
• Not preparing for class.
• Failing to ask questions.
• Relying on someone else's notes.
• Failing to improve performance.
• Developing a dislike for the class.

It is easy to maintain a strong academic record. However, if you find yourself having difficulty, seek help immediately! Many students wait until it is too late to ask for help. A good place to start is with your instructor. If he cannot adequately help you, consult academic support services on campus.

Questions

1. Why should you be concerned about your academic performance?
2. What things can you do to effectively manage your time?
3. Where is the best place to study?
4. How long should you study one subject at one time?
5. What does TQLR mean? How do you use it?
6. Describe a good way to take notes.
7. How should you prepare for an exam?
8. What should you do during an exam?
9. What should you do after an exam?
10. Describe some techniques in handling test anxiety.
11. What resources are available on your campus to help you with scholarship?
12. Give some warning signs that indicate potential for poor scholarship.

Essays

1. What is your personal goal for your grades this term? Next term? What is your Phikeia class' goal?
2. Why is scholarship so important in the Fraternity?

VIII

Symbols & Insignia

There are many things that separate Phi Delta Theta from other Greek organizations. Our symbols, rituals, and other sacred objects are shared only by members of our Fraternity. Through them we express our mutual devotion to Phi Delta Theta, and we recognize each other as true members of our great Fraternity.

The first Phi Delta Theta badge was made in June, 1849, and adopted by the Alpha chapter in the same month. It consisted of a flat gold shield with a scroll in the lower part bearing the Greek letters ΦΔΘ, and an eye in the upper portion. Morrison suggested the shield and eye, and Wilson the scroll. Though the badges were privately worn at Miami, and publicly in other places, they were not displayed at the University until June 26, 1852, when they were worn at a party given for the senior class by the president of Miami University, Dr. William C. Anderson,

himself an honorary member of Phi Delta Theta.

Beginning in 1866, a sword attached to the shield by a chain was commonly worn, but the attachment was not officially a part of the badge until it was formally adopted by the Convention of 1871. The badge, except as to size and ornamentation, has not been changed since then. The sword and shield make a unique and distinctive emblem. Though other fraternities have shield-shaped badges, none except Sigma Tau Gamma (1920) has ever had an attachment similar to the sword. The combination of sword and shield makes a badge which, even at a distance, is readily recognized.

The badge of the Fraternity is made of gold or platinum, and consists of a shield, with a scroll bearing the letters of Phi Delta Theta over the fesse and nonbril points, an eye over the honor point, and a sword attached by a chain from the sinister chief point to the hilt. The badge may be jewelled, and the scroll may be enamelled in white and the

---

Facing Page: Pallas Athena, the Ancient Greeks' goddess of wisdom, is Phi Delta Theta's tutelary divinity.

eye in black.

The sword shall always be worn with the shield, and both may be made in one piece, the sword appearing to pass diagonally back of the shield from the sinister chief point to the dexter base point. Every member shall wear the badge at all times appropriate. The proper place for it is over the heart rather than on the coat lapel.

THE SWORD & SHIELD.

The Code provides that the badge shall not be worn except by initiated members of the Fraternity or their mothers, wives, daughters, sisters, or fiancées, and a penalty of one year's suspension from the Fraternity may be imposed by a chapter on the member violating the clause.

Fraternity Insignia

The Phikeia Button. The first Phikeia button, adopted in 1894, was the first pledge button to be used by any fraternity. The present pledge pin was designed in 1900. It is a square with rounded corners with a white diagonal bar across it bearing the Greek word Φικεια. Above and below the bars are two blue fields with three gold stars in each field.

Coat of Arms. The present coat of arms was adopted in 1898. The shield is blue with a diagonal silver bar bearing a gold sword and three silver stars above and below the bar; a gold helmet with closed visor; mantling of blue and silver; the crest; a right arm, armored, hurling a javelin; the open motto on a riband below the shield.

The Open Motto. The open motto, Εις ανηρ ουδεις ανηρ (Eis aner oudeis aner), was adopted in 1880 and means literally, "One man is no man," or more freely interpreted,

"We enjoy life by the help and society of others."

Colors. The Fraternity colors, azure and argent (heraldic terms for blue and white), were chosen in 1871.

The Fraternity Flag. The flag was first used in 1889 and consisted of three white stars on a blue field. Its present form was suggested by Walter B. Palmer and adopted in 1896. It consists of three vertical bars of equal width; each of the outer bars is charged with three white five-pointed stars; the middle bar is charged with the letters ΦΔΘ in blue, reading downward; the width of the flag is two-thirds the length.

Fraternity and Chapter Banners. The Fraternity banner was first printed on the cover of THE SCROLL in 1884. The form now in use, adopted in 1896, is triangular, and bears across the body the word "Miami" over the figures "1848," with a Φ in the upper left, a Δ in the lower corner, and a Θ in the upper right. The body is blue, the lettering is gold. The standard bar, cord, and tassels are silvered.

The chapter banner is of the same design as the Fraternity banner except that for "Miami" and "1848" are substituted the name or initials of the college or university where the chapter was established and the year in which the chapter was chartered.

Fraternity Seal. Adopted in 1898, the seal consists of the escutcheon of the coat of arms, with the legend: "Great Seal of Phi Delta Theta Fraternity," and the figures "1848" in a circle around it.

Flower. The white carnation was adopted as the Fraternity flower in 1891.

Legion Buttons and Charms. The Silver Legion recognition button consists of the coat-of-arms in silver above which are displayed the words "Silver Legion" and the number "25." Similarly, the Golden Legion button is gold, diamond in shape and displays the coat of arms with a "5" and "0" to either side.

Every five years after the Golden Legion anniversary, an alumnus receives a charm recognizing the number of years he has been a Phi. The charm, which attaches to the Golden Legion button, is in the shape of an owl and displays ΦΔΘ and the number of years the alumnus has been a Phi.

The Diamond Legion charm is like the other charms, but is gold and displays the number "75". The Diamond Legion was established in 1992 and honors those men who have been Phis for 75 years or more.

The alumnus charm. The alumnus charm is of the same design as the pledge button, except that the Greek letters ΦΔΘ replace the word Φικεια.

The recognition button. A small gold, silver, or platinum button in the form of the coat of arms is the badge of recognition. It is used to recognize undergraduates or alumni who have achieved something exceptional for the Fraternity.

Pallas and Her Owl. Pallas Athena, the Ancient Greek's goddess of wisdom, is the tutelary goddess of Phi Delta Theta. The owl, which the Greeks regarded as sacred to her, is a symbol of the Fraternity.

The Badge of Mourning. Adopted in 1872, the badge of mourning consists of black-and-white crepe worn under the badge.

Convention Ladders. Many years ago, members who attended the General Conventions started the practice of wearing small silver bars to designate the number of conventions which they had attended. These bars, when linked together, resemble ladders. The wearers are called laddermen, and their lengthening ladders, as the years go by, are striking evidence of their devotion to the Fraternity. Each ladder bar indicates the city and year in which the convention took place.

Use of Fraternity Symbols

By tradition, the several symbols of Phi Delta Theta, even though public in nature, have been zealously guarded by the members. Most symbols are protected by the United States and Canadian copyright registration, and there are several sections of the Constitution and General Statutes pertaining to the use of symbols. For example, the General Statutes prohibit the manufacture of any articles bearing the badge design unless specifically authorized by the General Convention. The General Statutes also provide that the use of the coat of arms, badge, or other symbols of the Fraternity in such a way as to bring discredit to the organization shall be

"Fraternity Insignia"

PHIKEIA BUTTON.
Adopted, 1894.

ORIGINAL BADGE.
Founder Andrew
Watts Rogers.

COAT OF ARMS.
Adopted, 1898.

FRATERNITY FLAG.
Adopted, 1898.

grounds for disciplinary action against the offending member. All Fraternity symbols should be treated with respect. They should never be carved, engraved, or written in public places where they would attract attention. Chapters and individuals should use the name of the Fraternity only when engaged in proper activities. The name of the Fraternity should never be used for personal gain, and the General Statutes forbid the use of the name of the Fraternity or the name of a chapter in connection with any business enterprise.

Chapter Grand

The Chapter Grand is reserved for those Phis who have passed away. A list of obituaries about recently deceased Phis is published in each issue of THE SCROLL.

The Fraternity epitaph is *In coelo quies est,* translated, "In Heaven there is rest." The epitaph is printed at the end of the Chapter Grand section of THE SCROLL magazine.

Fraternity Publications

The Fraternity publishes many items, including PHIS SING, a compilation of the most popular songs of the Fraternity edited by David Turner, *Minnesota '70* (see Chapter XII). The Fraternity also publishes officer manuals for alumni and undergraduate officers, The Code of the Fraternity (see Chapter XIII,) this Phikeia Manual, a quarterly magazine, THE SCROLL, and a History of the Fraternity.

THE SCROLL of Phi Delta Theta is the second oldest fraternity journal. It was provided for by the Convention of 1873, and the first number, bearing the date of January, 1875, was published in the autumn of 1874. It contained three departments, fraternity, alumni, and literary, and was printed in Indianapolis. Seven numbers were published in magazine format through 1876. The editor and business

manager, taking all financial responsibility, then found that they could no longer carry the load, and publication was suspended for two years. It was resumed in September, 1878, with the General Fraternity backing it financially, and has been maintained continuously to the present time. The dates of issue have been changed from time to time; at present it is published in fall, winter, spring, and summer. Chapter newsletters, brief annual reports from each chapter, are published in each edition.

Between September 1878, and October 1880, THE SCROLL was a three-column monthly newspaper. Since then it has always been in the form of a magazine. The earlier volumes limited circulation to members of the Fraternity; this limitation was removed in 1881.

As the organ of Phi Delta Theta, THE SCROLL presents material of interest to college men in general and Phis in particular. Sketches of alumni and undergraduates who have distinguished themselves in various fields, contributions by experts on a variety of college issues, summaries of achievements in scholarship pursuits, sports, and other fields of student interest, reviews of books by Phi authors, are among the regular features in THE SCROLL. News from the chapters and alumni clubs are also popular features. THE SCROLL is an important means of unifying the Fraternity and maintaining the loyal interest of the alumni.

Walter B. Palmer, past president of the General Council, wrote the first history of the Fraternity, printed in 1906. It contains a foreword by Founder John Wolfe Lindley and more than 900 pages of chronological history. To recognize the 125th anniversary of the founding of Phi Delta Theta, the General Council commissioned Walter E. Havighurst, *Ohio Wesleyan '23,* to write a history which first appeared as an inset in THE

Scroll during the 1972–74 biennium. The document was later bound and released in book form under the title From Six at First, A History of Phi Delta Theta, 1848–1973. For the Fraternity's 150th anniversary celebration, Ritter Collett commemorated the history of the Fraternity when he published In the Bond.

The fraternity also communicates to members via the internet. Phi Delta Theta's presence on the web began in 1995. The site can be accessed at www.phideltatheta.org. The site contains information, e-mail links to General Headquarters, and other useful materials including a member forum.

Ritual

Part of the chapter experience is the weekly performance of certain ritual ceremonies. The members hold the ritual in high regard and practice it with great solemnity because it represents the heart of the Fraternity. Our ritual, like all other ceremonial rites, reaffirms our belief in and dedication to the principles on which the Fraternity was founded.

Ritual can become a repetitive drudgery for those who do not understand the values behind it. For that reason, members of the Fraternity should constantly seek to understand the tenets that are the basis of Phi Delta Theta. Once that understanding is achieved, ritual becomes a celebration of these values and a way to bring the brotherhood together for a common purpose.

Except for The Bond, that sacred document that every Phi must accept before becoming a member, the ritual is the only common experience that all Phis share. It is a mutual exercise that binds all members together in an international brotherhood.

Questions

1. Describe the badge of Phi Delta Theta.
2. Who designed the badge?
3. When was the badge first worn in public?
4. How is the badge to be worn, and who may wear it?
5. Describe the coat of arms.
6. What is the open motto? Its literal translation? Its more free interpretation?
7. What are the Fraternity colors? The Fraternity Flower?
8. Describe the Fraternity flag.
9. Who is the tutelary goddess of the Fraternity? What is her significance?
10. What is the Fraternity epitaph? What is the Chapter Grand?
11. What is the Silver Legion? The Golden Legion? The Diamond Legion?
12. Name the publications of the Fraternity.

Essay

1. What is the importance of ritual in the chapter?

IX

"The idea, of course, is to spur every undergraduate to greater action, which, after all, is for his own good. Better chapter, better men; that is one of the main objects back of the fraternity idea."
GEORGE BANTA JR., WABASH '14

Awards for Excellence

WHAT IS AN ideal chapter of a college Fraternity? An ideal chapter is one that is a credit to the university in which it is located, a credit to the Fraternity to which it belongs, and a credit to itself. To meet this test, the chapter must uplift the social, moral, and intellectual life of the university.

Each member should represent the values and principles of the Fraternity. Each immoral act reflects upon the chapter and institution as well as on the man himself, and each individual in the chapter should be made to feel the responsibility he carries on his shoulders, because the chapter gets its reputation from the behavior of each individual.

The chapter members should pride themselves on high scholastic achievement. Every member should realize that he is in college primarily for a quality education. A chapter is often judged by the faculty mainly on its scholarship standing, and individually, every man is judged on his attitude toward scholarship. The chapter should give hearty support to the faculty in all measures which look toward the improvement of individual and chapter character.

The ideal chapter may be defined as a harmonious brotherhood of college men working for the benefit of each other, the fraternity, and institution in which it is located, in social, moral, and intellectual life.

Although the feeling of achievement which accompanies successful chapter operation is in itself ample reward, the General Fraternity sponsors a system of awards recognizing excellence in various phases of chapter operation. All chapters are automatically considered in competition for some of the awards, while entry forms and substantiating information must be submitted for others. There are also a number of individual awards presented to Phis who have distinguished themselves in several areas. A few of these awards will be described in the following paragraphs.

Facing Page: Each year the General Fraternity honors chapters with awards for community service, Phikeia education, alumni programming and other areas of chapter organization.

Overall Excellence

Four trophies are presented annually to recognize all-around excellence in campus leadership, campus participation and internal chapter operations. The criteria used to categorize the chapters in Harvard, Founders, and Kansas City Trophy competition include the undergraduate male enrollment of the college or university, the number of fraternities on campus, and the total number of members in the chapter.

The chapter awards chairman must submit a detailed report to compete for these three trophies. The selection of winners is based on group scholarship; the recognition of individual members by virtue of their selection for membership in honor, recognition and professional societies; chapter and individual efforts in athletics; member participation in campus publications and student government; and chapter participation in general campus activities and community service.

Permanent trophies engraved with the names of the recipients are presented to the winners to be retained for a period of one year. Attractive wall plaques are also presented as a permanent record of achievement.

The Housser Trophy is awarded annually to the Canadian chapter which best meets criteria based on scholarship, internal administration, finance, community service, and performance of the ritual. The original trophy was an Inuit soapstone carving and was presented by the Vancouver Alumni Club in honor of George E. Housser, *McGill '06*, president of the General Council 1950-52. A replacement trophy, also an Inuit sculpture, was presented by the alumni of Canada at the 1992 Convention. The new trophy is on permanent display at the General Headquarters.

Gold & Silver Stars

Each year, the General Fraternity recognizes certain of its chapters which have experienced significant success in all areas of chapter operation. Such chapters are given the Gold Star Award for excellence or the Silver Star Award for honorable mention. The criteria for both awards are essentially the same and include chapter scholarship, promptness in submitting all required reports, sound financial operation, participation in Community Service Day, effective alumni relations, proper use of the ritual, and an educational Phikeia program.

In addition, the Improvement Citation recognizes chapters who have made significant improvement in at least three areas of chapter operation. Embossed certificates mounted on wood plaques are presented as awards in these categories.

General Headquarters Trophy

Arthur R. Priest, *DePauw 1891*, for many years the executive secretary of Phi Delta Theta, saw the need for the recognition of merit among the chapters for their cooperation with General Headquarters. In 1929, he presented to the Fraternity the General Headquarters Trophy which is presented annually to the chapter or chapters which accumulate 100 points as a result of submitting all reports and fees promptly. Each chapter is automatically in competition for the award and the judging is based solely on the receipt of all reports and payments by the deadlines established for the award. The chapter officers principally responsible for winning this award are the president, vice president, treasurer, and historian. A reasonably good record in accumulating points for this award is a prerequisite to being recognized for a number of other awards as outlined in this chapter.

Recognition of Scholarship

The General Fraternity recognizes two areas of chapter scholastic achievement annually in the form of attractively embossed certificates.

One is the Scholarship Award presented to chapters whose members achieve a the top grade point ranking in comparison with other campus fraternities. This competition is based on reports prepared locally by a representative of the host institution or by the Interfraternity Council. The other award is the Sound Learning Award which is judged on the basis of a written report submitted by the chapter describing its basic program of study hours, study groups, tutors, scholarship resource programs, recognition of members, high scholastic achievement, and innovative programs which encourage better learning and study habits.

Fraternity Education Award

The St. Louis Fraternity Education Trophy was presented to the Fraternity by the St. Louis Alumni Club during the 1982 Convention in that city. The award recognizes, on an annual basis, the chapter judged to have the most outstanding program for the education and indoctrination of Phikeias and the entire membership. The attractive trophy is retained by the chapter for a period of one year, and a permanent wall plaque is also presented.

Bininger Religious Life Award

The Bininger Religious Life Trophy, presented by Dr. and Mrs. Clem E. Bininger, *Centre '31*, is awarded annually to the chapter whose members best seek to develop on their campus the type of moral character and religious service contemplated in The Bond. Chapter officers must submit an entry form with substantiating documents to compete for the trophy. Criteria include the quality of ritualistic activities within the chapter, the nature of the chapter's Founders Day observance, the

HARVARD AND FOUNDERS TROPHIES.
Annual chapter awards, like these trophies, are presented at General Convention or Leadership College.

chapter's efforts to improve the character of chapter members, the individual and chapter religious activities, and the general reputation of the chapter on campus and in the community, as evidenced by supplementary letters from campus officials, the Province President and the chapter advisory board chairman.

Community Service Awards

Each year, Phi Delta Theta sponsors the month of April for community service with the following purposes: (1) to encourage efforts of active chapters to help improve their surrounding community, (2) to demonstrate to the public some of the values of fraternity life, (3) to strengthen the chapter by working together for one common goal, (4) to put into action the principles of our great Fraternity. This program was initiated in 1955 through the efforts of Stanley D. Brown, *Nebraska-UCLA '36*, who later became president of the General Council.

Chapter officers must submit documentation to be eligible for the community service awards. The Beam Trophy for the activity judged to be the outstanding philanthropic project was presented to the Fraternity by the Des Moines Alumni Club in memory of Paul C. Beam, *Indiana-Illinois '22*, Executive Secretary from 1937–55. The Lubbock Trophy, donated by the Lubbock Alumni Club, is awarded annually to the undergraduate chapter which is judged to have been involved in the most significant continuing project carried out over an extended period. The Stan Brown Trophy recognizes the most outstanding one-day or individual project. In addition, Community Service Citations are presented to chapters which have distinguished themselves in community service activities.

Publication Awards

Three awards are presented each year that recognize chapters in the area of publications.

The William Allen White Trophy is presented to the chapter which produces the outstanding alumni newsletter. The award is named after the famous author, essayist, and newspaperman, William Allen White, *Kansas 1890*, who became known as the "Sage from Emporia."

A second award is given to the chapter which is judged to have prepared the best brochure written principally as a recruitment booklet or as an annual chapter yearbook. The third award is based on the best website among undergraduate chapters.

Dallas Alumni Award

The Dallas Award was donated by the alumni of that city to recognize the undergraduate chapter which best promotes continued involvement in the Fraternity among alumni.

Biggers Ritual Trophy

This trophy is awarded to the chapters that demonstrate quality ritual performances, practice the ritual on a weekly basis, and maintain proper ritual paraphernalia.

Phi Delta Theta Foundation Awards

The Phi Delta Theta Foundation offers more than 40 scholarships annually to men who are judged to be Phi Delta Theta's most outstanding undergraduates. Each chapter is urged to nominate its member who best exemplifies the teachings of The Bond. Accomplishments in the areas of scholarship, chapter service, campus activities and honors, as well as community involvement are considered by the judges. Rectitude, leadership and character are also important qualifications. The Arthur R. Priest Award is awarded to the nominee judged to be the best all-around candidate. The award is named in memory of the Fraternity's first Executive Secretary. Two Robert J. Miller Leadership Awards are presented in honor of the Fraternity's long-time Executive Vice President. The winners are the nominees who have demonstrated the most outstanding leadership in their chapter.

Harmon-Rice-Davis Trophy
At the 1956 Convention in Boulder, Colorado, Tom Harmon, *Michigan '41*, a former All-American football star, Heisman Trophy winner, and talented sports commentator on radio and television, noted that, among the Fraternity's many awards, there seemed to be a lack of recognition for athletic achievement. Brother Harmon presented a trophy, not in his name, but in the name of Grantland Rice, the internationally known sports writer. The name was changed to the Harmon-Rice Award in order to preserve the names of both

of these famed Phi figures from the world of sports. In 1991, the name of the trophy was again changed to add the name of Dr. John Davis Jr., *Washburn '38*, THE SCROLL's long-time sports editor.

The recipient of the Harmon-Rice-Davis Trophy must be more than just an excellent athlete. He is judged on the basis of his participation in chapter activities, his scholarship, and his contribution to the campus. A replica of the beautiful trophy is presented to the recipient as his personal award, while the large, permanent trophy is displayed at General Headquarters.

George M. Trautman Memorial Award
This award was created in honor of George M. Trautman, *Ohio State '14*, the late president

FOUNDATION SCHOLARSHIPS.
The Phi Delta Theta Educational Foundation and the Canadian Scholarship Foundation offer more than 65 grants and fellowships of up to $4,000 to undergraduate or graduate student Phis every year.

of the Association of Minor Leagues of Professional Baseball. During the nine years prior to his death in 1963, he served as chairman of the Lou Gehrig Memorial Award Committee. The Trautman award is presented to the undergraduate Phi who is judged to be the Fraternity's outstanding representative in college baseball.

Raymond L. Gardner Award

The Raymond L. Gardner "Alumnus of the Year" Award, is presented by the Seattle Alumni Club in memory of the Washington Phi who served as a member of the General Council. The award is presented in recognition of the individual's participation in Fraternity affairs, activities in higher education, and community service. To be eligible for this award, a Phi must be nominated by a chapter or alumni club of the Fraternity. A committee determines who will be the recipient each year.

Distinguished Alumnus Award

This award honors an alumnus for outstanding career achievement in his profession or in volunteer service. Involvement with the General Fraternity is not a criterion. More than one alumnus can receive the award each year, and a committee makes the selections based on nominations received during the year. The annual award was created in 1994 by the General Council.

Samuel V. Stone Award

The Samuel V. Stone Outstanding Chapter Advisory Board Chairman of the Year Award was presented to the Fraternity in recognition of the services rendered by the longtime adviser of the Texas Gamma Chapter at Southwestern University. It is awarded annually to the most outstanding chapter advisory board chairman in the Fraternity. Several criteria are used in selecting a recipient, including the

chairman's length of service and the general condition of the chapter as evidenced by the chapter's recognition, awards, and general operation. Nominations and applications for this award are submitted by the chapter to General Headquarters.

Nance-Millett Free Enterprise Award

The Nance-Millett Award was given to the Fraternity in 1980 by James J. Nance, *Ohio Wesleyan '23*, and past president of the General Council, John D. Millett, *DePauw '33*. It is presented every other year to an individual who has made an outstanding contribution to the free enterprise system. The candidate will preferably be a member of Phi Delta Theta, but membership in the Fraternity is not a prerequisite.

The recipient is invited to address a session of the General Convention, at which time the award is presented. Nominations for the award may be submitted to General Headquarters, and the selection is made by the General Council.

Legion of Honor & Merit

The Legion of Honor and Legion of Merit are the most prestigious awards an alumnus can receive. The Legion of Honor recognizes a member who: (1) has made a major contribution of his time, effort, and energy to serving the Fraternity and improving its stature; (2) has distinguished himself in representing the Fraternity's principles of friendship, sound learning and rectitude; (3) is widely recognized as a leader of fraternity men and identified with the promotion of fraternities, and (4) has widely advanced and enlarged the opportunities for growth and leadership among college men through fraternities.

The Legion of Merit is much like the Legion of Honor except that it places more emphasis on service to Phi Delta Theta and attaches less importance to interfraternity and community affairs. The individual who receives this recognition has rendered distinguished service to the Fraternity above and beyond the call of duty.

The General Council determines the recipients of these two awards and presents the awards at the Biennial Convention.

Lou Gehrig Memorial Award

There is one other award presented by the Fraternity which, more often than not, goes to a nonmember. The Lou Gehrig Memorial Award is granted annually by Phi Delta Theta to the major league baseball player who is judged to have exemplified in playing ability and personal character the attributes of the Hall of Fame first baseman of the New York Yankees. Lou Gehrig, Columbia '25, was four times voted the most valuable player in the American League, and established himself as the "Iron Horse" of baseball by setting the all-time major league mark of playing in 2,130 consecutive games.

Two Phis have received this award. Alvin Dark, *Louisiana State '45,* was awarded the original trophy in 1954. Ron Cey, *Washington State '70,* won the award in 1982. The permanent trophy is prominently displayed in the Baseball Hall of Fame at Cooperstown, New York. A replica of the trophy is presented during pregame activities in the host city of the player's club.

Questions

1. What are the characteristics of the ideal chapter?
2. What are the top four awards given to chapters each year? For which award is your chapter eligible?
3. What are the criteria for a Gold Star?
4. What is the General Headquarters Trophy?
5. What is the St. Louis Trophy?
6. What is the Bininger Religious Life Trophy?
7. Name the three service awards and the criteria of each.
8. What is the Harmon-Rice-Davis Trophy? For whom is it named?
9. What is the George M. Trautman Trophy?
10. Who is awarded the Samuel Stone Award?
11. What are the Legion of Honor and the Legion of Merit?
12. What is the Lou Gehrig Memorial Award? Name the Phis who have won it.

Essays

1. Which awards has your chapter won recently. Which awards would you like to see your chapter win?
2. Discuss a strategy for your chapter to win these awards.

X

"Fraternities are now on trial; not only that, but they are fighting on the defensive. The result has been to place all fraternities on their mettle to demonstrate to the world that they are worthwhile and are doing good work in promoting scholarship, morality, democracy, and college loyalty."
WALTER B. PALMER, EMORY-VANDERBILT 1877

Risk Management

RISK MANAGEMENT HAS become one of the most frequently discussed issues in the Greek world over the past fifteen years. Increasing concerns about alcohol consumption, hazing, and housing safety have led many Greek organizations to develop a series of policies that attempt to limit liability and increase the safety of their members. The concern has risen from the number of civil suits brought against Greek-letter organizations as a result of accidents at fraternity functions and on fraternity property. Guests injured in alcohol related accidents, members injured in unsafe housing, students hurt as a result of hazing activities... these events have led to much criticism of the Greek community as well as multi-million dollar lawsuits. These suits have forced many Greek organizations to obtain liability insurance and to reevaluate behavior within their undergraduate chapters.

Over the years, risk management has become a part of Greek life. Being conscious of potential risk is now a part of being in a fraternity. Undergraduate leaders are faced not only with the responsibility of ensuring the safety of guests, but ensuring the safety of their chapter brothers as well.

Broadly stated, risk management is understanding and recognizing potential hazards during chapter events and in the chapter facility and actively working to reduce the chances of an accident. At first glance this seems to be a matter of common sense, but for many chapters, managing risk is a constant battle. Most risks in a chapter involve alcohol, and many fraternities, including Phi Delta Theta, have developed educational programs and other policies such as alcohol-free housing to help educate their members about the dangers of abusing alcohol.

More than two-thirds of all accidents in or near a chapter facility are alcohol-related; eight in ten acts of campus violence are related to alcohol; nearly nine in ten sexual

---

Facing Page: Elliott Hall on the campus of Miami University. John McMillan Wilson's room is to the left of the plaque. This room is now named the Founders Room.

assaults on campus are alcohol-related. Although college students are warned repeatedly, there continue to be times when people drink and act irresponsibly, often endangering themselves and others. Alcohol affects judgment; drinking often leads to bad decisions. It is easy to see then that in order to successfully manage risk in a chapter, the proper management of alcohol consumption must be a priority.

Planning Social Activities

Managing alcohol consumption does not mean eliminating drinking altogether; however it does mean preventing people from drinking to the point of injury. Many chapters have an alcohol education program for the Phikeias and chapter membership. In addition, they make many preparations before any social event involving alcohol.

The Event Planning Program is designed to help chapters plan social events within the risk management guidelines. This program consists of an event planning form that is filled out by the chapter's risk management chairman and submitted to the director of risk management at General Headquarters for review. The review will result in helping to educate the chapter on ways to reduce the potential risk of the event. Whether the event is a date party using a third party vendor or a recruitment function, this program helps educate the members on the potential risks associated with the event and ensures compliance with the risk management policies.

Some of the areas covered by the event planning form include: event location, service of alcohol beverages, drunk driving prevention, security and transportation exposures, crisis management plans, and contractual exposures which are set up to reduce the chapter's liability even further by using hired third parties. While the risk of an accident can never be completely eliminated, following the risk management policies and using the event planning program can reduce the chances of an injury and limit the liability of the chapter. If your Phikeia class is planning a social event, work with the chapter's risk management chairman and review the event planning forms to help make your event safe and enjoyable.

Risk Management Policies

In 1990, Phi Delta Theta adopted a series of guidelines that govern the use of alcohol at chapter functions. These policies were created to help each chapter protect itself from liability and from the potential dangers of unrestricted alcohol use at Fraternity events. The policies also forbid hazing, as well as illegal drug use in the chapter, and encourage chapters to maintain a safe chapter house. If the policies are followed correctly, a chapter can dramatically reduce the chances of an accident, as well as protect itself and its members against a civil suit if an accident does occur.

In regard to alcohol, the policies stress several items:

• *The law must be followed.* No one under 21 years of age shall be allowed to drink at chapter events.

• *Chapter funds may not be used to purchase alcohol.* This includes "passing the hat" and having separate social accounts. All functions involving alcohol shall be strictly "invitation only," and chapters should use third party vendors to dispense beverages. Because the chapter is not providing or serving the alcohol, this rule limits the liability of the Fraternity.

• *Kegs, bulk quantities of alcohol, and public-access alcohol are prohibited.* Alcohol can be dangerous if it is not properly managed. Ensuring those of legal age are the only ones drinking and then monitoring their personal consumption is difficult in this scenario. Kegs and bulk quantities of alcohol can lead to

Risk Management Policies of Phi Delta Theta

Abusive Behavior. The Fraternity will not tolerate or condone any form of abusive behavior on the part of its members or Phikeias, whether physical, mental or emotional. This is to include any actions directed toward members or nonmembers. Fighting is not an acceptable form of behavior as a member of Phi Delta Theta.

Alcohol and Drugs

(1) All chapter facilities and properties in Phi Delta Theta Fraternity shall be alcohol-free at all times and under all circumstances. The implementation of these procedures is a continuation of the ongoing educational efforts of the General Fraternity.
(2) The possession, use and/or consumption of any alcoholic beverages by any Fraternity member, Phikeia, or guest, during chapter activities, or in any situation sponsored or endorsed by the chapter, *must* be in compliance with the laws and ordinances of the state, province, city, county, and university/college.
(3) No chapter of Phi Delta Theta may purchase alcoholic beverages with Fraternity funds, nor may any member or Phikeia in the name of or on behalf of the chapter coordinate the collections of any funds for such a purchase. This includes, but is not limited to, the following: the purchase of kegs, party balls, and other bulk quantities of alcoholic beverages.
(4) No chapter of Phi Delta Theta may co-sponsor or co-finance a function where alcohol is purchased by any of the host chapters, groups or organizations.
(5) The use or distribution of kegs or party balls by the chapter at chapter events is strictly forbidden.
(6) The sale of alcoholic beverages by any chapter of Phi Delta Theta is strictly forbidden. No chapter of Phi Delta Theta shall participate in any activity or action which creates the impression that the chapter is selling alcohol. Examples include, but are not limited to: charging admission to parties, passing the hat, selling empty cups, selling drink tickets, or having vending machines which dispense alcoholic beverages.
(7) The use or possession of any unlawful drug in any form is not permitted at any Phi Delta Theta function or in any Phi Delta Theta chapter facility.
(8) Parties and social activities should be open to members, Phikeias, and *invited guests only.* Open parties, meaning those with unrestricted access by nonmembers of the Fraternity, without specific invitation, are prohibited.
(9) All undergraduate recruitment functions and recruitment activities associated with or sponsored by any club/association of Phi Delta Theta will be alcohol-free.
(10) Alcoholic beverages are prohibited at any Phikeia program or initiation ceremony of the chapter.
(11) Chapters are strongly encouraged to conduct alcohol and drug awareness programs for members and Phikeias.

Hazing. No chapter or member of Phi Delta Theta shall indulge in any physical abuse or undignified treatment (hazing). Hazing is defined as: "any action taken or situation created, intentionally or unintentionally, whether on or off Fraternity premises, and whether with or without the consent of the persons subjected to the action, which produces mental or physical discomfort, embarrassment, harassment, or ridicule." Such activities and situations include: paddling in any form, creation of excessive fatigue, physical and psychological shocks, quests, treasure hunts, scavenger hunts, road trips, or any other such activities carried on outside the confines of the facility, wearing apparel in public which is conspicuous and not normally in good taste, engaging in any public stunts and buffoonery, morally degrading or humiliating games and activities, late work sessions which interfere with scholastic activity, and any other activities which are not consistent with fraternal law, ritual or policy with the regulations and policies of the educational institution.

High-Risk Events. Phi Delta Theta chapters cannot afford the exposure of sponsoring, organizing, endorsing or participating in events or activities which involve a high-risk of physical injury or damage to property. While no definitive list of such events can be given, chapters must take a common sense approach to evaluating the risk of a particular event or activity. Examples of high-risk events include, but are not limited to the following: bungee jumping, parachuting, athletic events such as boxing, roof-top functions, water skiing or other water-related activities, especially those activities which relate to any type of temporary pool or water slide.

Property Management. The chapter facility, along with its furnishings and landscape, should provide for each member an environment for study, clean and safe living conditions, and recreational facilities. A sound program focused on proper maintenance of the property, along with due regard for university/college, health, or fire department regulations, where applicable, shall be followed in each chapter.

Transportation. Phi Delta Theta chapters are encouraged to establish a transportation policy for chapter events which are not held at or within walking distance from the chapter facility. It is strongly recommended that the policy include the use of a form of mass transportation, such as charter buses, to transport members for such events, and particularly for events where alcohol may be consumed. When mass transportation is not available, alternative procedures, such as designated drivers, should be used.

Issued by the General Council of Phi Delta Theta Fraternity (November 10, 2000).
The Risk Management Policies of Phi Delta Theta are intended to provide education and guidance to chapter officers in performing their responsibilities. Individual chapter members and officers are responsible for being familiar with these policies.

mass consumption which then can lead to other dangerous activities such as drinking and driving, date rape, and assaults.

• *Recruitment activities must be alcohol-free.* All Greek councils on your campus have similar policies. Recruiting potential members without alcohol will attract a greater number of high quality rushees, and improve the retention ratio of new members. Show potential members the benefits of being a member of Phi Delta Theta. Brotherhood activities and other events allow for opportunities to interact and get to know potential members. Also remember serving alcohol to minors is illegal and will open you to the risk of potential legal liability and property damage.

Each Phikeia and member should read the complete risk management policies outlined on the preceding page in this chapter. If you have questions regarding the policy be sure to ask the Phikeia educator or the chapter's risk management chairman for clarification.

Alcohol-free Housing Policy

As of July 1, 2000 alcoholic beverages are not allowed in chapter facilities. The General Council made an historic decision to implement this policy in February of 1997. Their goal was to combat the alcohol-dominated culture and to assist chapters in returning to the basic principles of fraternity life.

Phi Delta Theta is leading the Greek world with the development of this policy and has received many allocades from alumni, university administrators, and other fraternity leaders for taking this bold step. Those chapters that have embraced the policy have seen a rise in their overall scholastic ranking, an increase in the number pledged and initiated, and great improvements in the cleanliness and

LEARNING AT LEADERSHIP COLLEGE.
Undergraduate Phis come to Miami University each year to learn about a variety of campus issues like risk management.

safety of their chapter facilities. These chapters have also seen increased interest and support from their alumni.

Chapter Annexes

Many members in your chapter may live outside of the chapter facility and often hold social gatherings which usually include members from the chapter. Although it is difficult to determine whether these activities should be deemed official chapter events, you should still be aware of the potential risks associated with such activities.

Phi Delta Theta has been involved in lawsuits where events have been held at residences where members of the Fraternity reside. Breaking Fraternity policy such as having large quantities of alcohol including kegs or allowing underage consumption at these events jeopardizes the chapter's charter. When these types of activities occur, remember the risk management policies of Phi Delta Theta must be followed at all times.

Alcohol 101

This interactive CD-ROM program has been used as part of the continuing alcohol education efforts of the Fraternity. The program provides a variety of information in a user friendly, video game type interaction.

Alcohol 101 is designed to allow members and Phikeias to be open and honest while examining the risks associated with their own personal drinking behavior. The program compares the users own drinking habits with the social norms allowing them to explore various bits of beneficial information at their own pace and order.

A copy of Alcohol 101 has been sent to every chapter and can be obtained from the Phikeia educator or the chapter president.

Fraternity Insurance Policy

The General Fraternity has a liability insurance policy which covers all undergraduate chapters, the undergraduate members, and alumni officers of the Fraternity while conducting Fraternity business. Coverage could be voided if the chapter violates the risk management policies or the law is not followed.

Every undergraduate chapter must pay a prorated premium each year to pay for the cost of the insurance policy. The premium is based on the individual chapter's size and the chapter's claims history among other various items.

The policy was established in 1985. Since that time, various claims have been filed with the insurance underwriters. As a result, several chapters in Phi Delta Theta have been involved in a liability claim. Although many people feel that the chances of an accident occurring are slim, the facts indicate if alcohol is involved and precautionary steps are not taken, the likelihood of an accident occurring is great.

Fraternities are among the highest risk groups with regard to liability, and adequate insurance coverage can be obtained only at a high premium and by establishing and enforcing policies to reduce risk. Without the Fraternity's risk management policies, every chapter of Phi Delta Theta would be left without liability insurance.

Personal Responsibility

Risk management may seem like more trouble than it is worth, and it may seem as if it infringes on the free-flowing social atmosphere that college life brings, but risk management is quite simply a way to avoid what could potentially be a disastrous situation. No one wants to bother with policing the chapter social events, but no one wants to end up responsible for an injury either.

It is well to remember that we are our brothers' keepers. Although there may be times when managing risk is not the most popular course of action, remember being responsible is more an issue of safety than an issue of popularity.

Remember also that personal responsibility means each individual member is responsible for his behavior. Irresponsible, dangerous, reckless, or illegal acts have no place in Phi Delta Theta, and they should be immediately addressed by chapter leaders.

Risk management has helped all Greek organizations to recommit themselves to the principles upon which they were founded. Although the Founders of Phi Delta Theta avoided alcohol altogether, their conviction to act responsibly, intelligently, and with goodwill is still applicable in today's more socially liberal culture. All members should keep in mind the tenets of The Bond and our founding principles in their daily activities. Encouraging and demonstrating responsible behavior is just a modern extension of the Fraternity's basic precepts. Being a mature person and a good Phi means adopting this philosophy.

Life Safety

One aspect of risk management which is commonly overlooked is life safety. This is an important issue no matter where you reside and one you should be concerned about even after college. Life safety means working with your chapter brothers to ensure your living facility meets or exceeds local fire codes. Local fire marshalls will often inspect your property for free and will help you develop plans on how to react during a real fire.

Phi Delta Theta is no stranger to chapter facility fires. As pictured below, the Mississippi Alpha chapter lost their house to arson. Fortunately, it was during the summer months when school was not in session and no one was seriously hurt. The Ohio Beta chapter was not as fortunate when they lost the life of a brother from a fire which started from smoldering cigar ashes in a couch.

More and more chapter facility fires have occurred over the last five years than in recent

FIRE! THE MISSISSIPPI ALPHA CHAPTER LOSES THEIR HOUSE IN 1996.
You think it won't happen, but you should be prepared if it does. Fraternity house fires have claimed too many lives.

memory. On graduation day, five people died in a fire in the Phi Gamma Delta chapter facility at UNC-Chapel Hill. Smoldering smoking materials or a carelessly discarded match started the blaze amid clutter and trash stacked under the bar after a social event that evening. All fraternities continually battle to educate undergraduates on how to protect themselves and their property from fires.

Several major contributions to fraternity fire tragedies include: non-sprinklered buildings, fire extinguishers and smoke detectors stolen, broken, or tampered with by guests or occupants, overload of electrical circuits with TVs, stereos, and computers, party guests coming and going at all hours with little or no supervision, generally poor housekeeping, doors and windows left open around the clock, make-shift wooden lofts, lack of appropriate fire walls, fire doors, lighted exit signs, and less than adequate means of escape from all rooms and floors.

Phi Delta Theta and their insurance broker James R. Favor & Company have partnered to inspect each chapter facility every three years. Results are sent to the chapter's house corporation for follow-up. This has helped to identify problem areas so they can be corrected before another tragedy. Leadership Consultants also personally inspect each facility during their routine visits to your chapters.

There are several things each undergraduate can do to prevent chapter facility fires. Setting up designated smoking areas, posting fire evacuation routes in each room, having semesterly or quarterly fire drills, securing the property each night, performing monthly fire and safety inspections, not allowing fire doors to be wedged open, and assigning regular housekeeping duties cost nothing but are effective in preventing fires. Ask your house corporation or risk management chairman how you can help.

Questions

1. What is risk management?
2. Why has risk management become such a big issue in Greek organizations?
3. How does alcohol play a part in risk management?
4. When were the risk management policies created? What were some of the modifications made over the years?
5. Why did the General Council institute the alcohol-free housing policy?
6. What insurance coverages are afforded to you and when are they in effect?
7. Approximately what fraction of chapters have had a liability insurance claim?
8. What are the policies regarding hazing?
9. What is the definition of life safety?
10. What action can you take to help protect your chapter from a fire?
11. What precautions should a chapter take before a party involving alcohol?
12. What risks are associated with having chapter annexes?

Essays

1. Why do you think the chapter should be responsible for its guests as well as members?
2. Use the event planning program and mock up a detailed plan for your Phikeia class social event.

XI

"I believe that the message of Apollo XI was that in the spirit of Apollo, a free and open spirit, you can attack a very difficult goal and achieve it, if you can all agree and work together to achieve that goal."

NEIL ARMSTRONG, PURDUE '55

Famous Phis

ALUMNI OF Phi Delta Theta have distinguished themselves in virtually every field of endeavor. Nearly 800 Phis were recorded in a recent edition of WHO'S WHO IN AMERICA, more than any other fraternity. More than 20 Phis have earned Gold Medals at the Olympics. More than 100 Phis have served in the U.S. federal government, and more than 200 Phis have played in the NFL.

Phi Delta Theta's most prominent member was Benjamin Harrison, *Miami (Ohio) 1852*, president of the United States from 1889–93. Adlai E. Stevenson, *Centre 1860*, served as vice president of the United States from 1893–97. William B. Bankhead, *Alabama 1893*, was Speaker of the House of Representatives from 1934–41.

Phis continue to hold prominent government positions and have included Senators Samuel A. Nunn, J. Bennett Johnston; Representatives James Ramstad, and Joel M. Hefley.

Perhaps the most famous alumni in the Fraternity are those who made such lasting contributions to the world that they have earned a place in the public's memory. They have become legendary.

Lou Gehrig, *Columbia '25*, was the immortal first baseman for the New York Yankees who ended his career when he was afflicted with ALS. Many of his records in professional baseball still stand, including his 2,130 consecutive games played which earned him the nickname "Iron Horse."

Frank Lloyd Wright, *Wisconsin 1889*, became the world's most famous architect. He created many innovations in modern architecture, including the famous "prairie style." The Guggenheim Museum in New York City is perhaps his most familiar work.

Neil Armstrong, *Purdue '55*, was the commander of Apollo XI and the first man on the moon. The success of his mission marked the height of the U.S. space program and became a monument to mankind's achievement.

Facing Page: Lou Gehrig, *Columbia '25*, sits out his first game in 2,130 consecutive starts for the Yankees, 1939. He never played again, but his record remains.

ROBERT ALLEN
Wabash '57
Chairman, AT&T

WILLIAM W. ALLEN
Oklahoma State '56
CEO Phillips Petroleum

JAMES A. BAKER III
Texas '57
Former Secretary of State

GARY BENDER
Wichita '62
Television Sportscaster

DIRK BENEDICT
Whitman '67
Actor

JERRY BEST
Michigan State '59
President, Omni Hotels

BILL BIXBY
California '56
Actor & Director

RICH BROOKS
Oregon State '63
Football Coach, Oregon

GEORGE BUSBEE
Georgia '50
Former Georgia Governor

RON CEY
Washington State '70
Former L.A. Dodger

DABNEY COLEMAN
Texas '53
Actor

BARBER CONABLE
Cornell '43
Pres., World Bank

TIM CONWAY
Bowling Green '56
Actor & Comedian

JAMES H. DAUGHDRILL
Davidson '56
Pres., Rhodes College

CLIFF DOCHTERMAN
Ohio Wesleyan '47
Past President of Rotary
International

TERRY DORNBUSH
Vanderbilt '55
U.S. Ambassador to the
Netherlands

NEIL ARMSTRONG, *Purdue '55,* Commander of Apollo XI and first man on the Moon.

WILLIAM B. BANKHEAD, Alabama 1893, Speaker of the U.S. House of Representatives, 1934–41.

ROGER EBERT
Illinois '64
Film Critic

WEEB EWBANK
Miami (Ohio) '28
Former NFL Coach

JOHN TRAYNOR EYTON
Toronto '56
Canadian Senator

GEORGE M.C. FISHER
Illinois '62
CEO, Eastman Kodak

THOMAS FRIST
Vanderbilt '60
Hospital Co. of America

BOOTH GARDNER
Washington '58
Fmr. Washington Gov.

JACK HAM
Penn State '71
NFL Hall of Fame

TOM HARMON
Michigan '41
1940 Heisman-winner

JOEL HEFLEY
Oklahoma State '59
U.S. Representative

WAYLAND HOLYFIELD
Arkansas '64
Songwriter

GEN. CHARLES HORNER
Iowa '58
Cmdr. NORAD

RAY L. HUNT
Southern Methodist '65
Pres., Hunt Oil Co.

CARL JAMES
Duke '51
Big 8 Conference
Commissioner

F. ROSS JOHNSON
Manitoba '52
Fmr. CEO, RJR Nabisco

J. BENNETT JOHNSON
Washington & Lee '54
U.S. Senator

HANK KETCHUM
Washington '41
Cartoonist creator of
"Dennis the Menace."

MICHAEL KIRBY
Dalhousie '61
Canadian Senator

CHARLES KNAPP
Iowa State '68
Pres., Univ. of Georgia

J. WILLARD MARRIOTT
Utah '25
Founder, Marriott Hotels

JOHN McLAMORE
Cornell '42
Founder of Burger King

JASON McMANUS
Davidson '56
Editor-in-Chief, *Time*

F. STORY MUSGRAVE
Syracuse '58
NASA Astronaut

SAM NUNN
Georgia Tech '60
U.S. Senator

JIM OTTO
Miami (Fla.) '60
NFL Hall of Fame

BILLY PAYNE
Georgia '69
Pres. '96 Olympic Comm.

REYNOLDS PRICE
Duke '55
Author

DONALD PRIGMORE
Kansas State '54
Pres., GTE Sprint

JIM RAMSTAD
Minnesota '7
U.S. Representative

BURT REYNOLDS
Florida State '57
Actor

GRANTLAND RICE
Vanderbilt '01
Famed Sportswriter

BOB SCHIEFFER
Texas Christian '59
CBS News Anchor

DETLEF SCHREMPF
Washington '84
NBA All-Star

BENJAMIN HARRISON, *Miami 1852*, 23rd President of the United States, 1889–93.

C. J. SILAS
Georgia Tech '53
CEO, Phillips Petroleum*

JOHN SMALE
Miami '49
CEO, Procter & Gamble*

ROGER SMITH
Michigan '52
Fmr. Chairman of GM

ADLAI STEVENSON
Centre 1860
U.S. Vice President, 1893-97

WILLIAM STYRON
Davidson '47
Author

STEVE TASKER
Northwestern '84
NFL All-Pro

BILL TOOMEY
Colorado '61
'68 Olympic Gold Medal

JIM WACKER
Valparaiso '59
Coach, U. of Minnesota

PHIL WALDEN
Mercer '62
Pres. Capricorn Records

DOAK WALKER
Southern Methodist '50
NFL Hall of Fame

WILLIAM WEISS
Penn State '51
Fmr. CEO Ameritech

WILLIAM A. WHITE
Kansas 1890
Author & Essayist

MARK WHITE
Baylor '62
Fmr. Texas Governor

RALPH WILSON
Virginia '40
Owner, Buffalo Bills

WILLIAM WINTER
Mississippi '44
Fmr. Mississippi
Governor

RON WOODARD
Puget Sound '65
Pres., Boeing
Commercial

*Former CEO and chairman

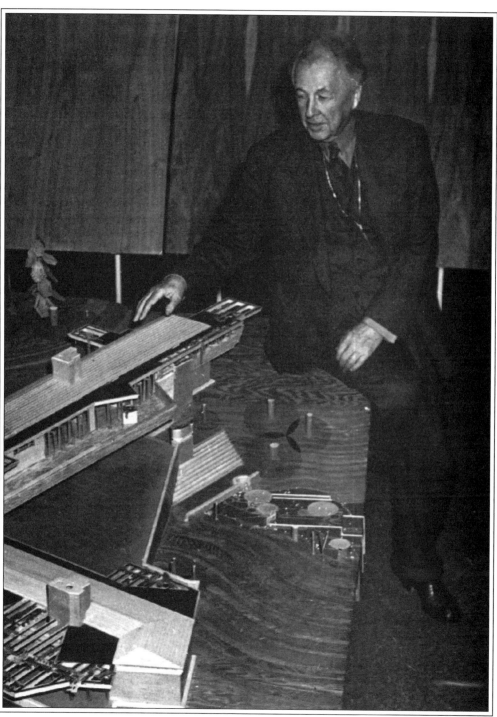

Frank Lloyd Wright, *Wisconsin 1889,* world-renowned architect and artist.

XII

We meet tonight with mirth and song
The evening hours to speed,
To burnish bright our sword and shield
For use in time of need;
Again we promise to protect
Each loyal brother knight,
And pray the God of grace to bless
Our army for the right.
GEN. JOHN CHARLES BLACK, WABASH 1864

Songs of Phi Delta Theta

IN 1866, AT THE installation of the Illinois Beta Chapter at the University of Chicago, one of the chapter's founders, General John Charles Black, *Wabash 1864*, introduced the first song composed for the Fraternity. The song (see above) was titled "Our Army for the Right, Boys."

After the enthusiastic reception of General Black's song, other Phis began to write lyrics about Phi Delta Theta to popular tunes of the day, and singing became a traditional part of the Fraternity. Eventually, Phi Delta Theta even came to be known as the "Singing Fraternity."

Like the Phis of old, members of many chapters engage in singing the songs of Phi Delta Theta, whether it is at formal occasions, during ritual ceremonies, at serenades, or just during the camaraderie of brotherhood. Several chapters also participate in interfraternity or intramural choral competitions.

The songs that are included in this Manual are the more frequently sung melodies of Phi Delta Theta and are used on a variety of occasions. Phikeias should take time during the pledge program to rehearse and perform these songs.

Phi Delta Theta publishes a compilation of all of the songs of the Fraternity called PHIS SING. A cassette with musical accompaniment is also offered through General Headquarters to easily teach the songs of the Fraternity to members.

Although singing has always been a significant part of being a part of Phi Delta Theta, singing in chapters does not occur as frequent as it once did. It has been said that "a good chapter is a singing chapter," perhaps because singing is one way of truly demonstrating the feeling of brotherhood.

In addition to the songs of Phi Delta Theta, a Phikeia should learn the songs of his university or college. Learning these songs and singing them demonstrates pride in the institution and pride in the Fraternity.

University of Akron Phis perform songs of the Fraternity at the 1956 General Convention in Boulder, Colorado.

Opening Ceremony Song

Old Hundredth

Alternate text:

Hail to the golden Shield we wear!
Hail to the gleaming Sword so fair!
Hail to the spotless white and blue!
Hail to the Brotherhood so true!

Clarence Jacob Reddig, Gettysburg, '77

Warrior Greeks of Old

George Wilson Van Gorder, Williams '11

"Army Blue"
Setting: Chester L. Alwes, Hanover '69

1. Once when war - rior Greek met Greek, Back in the days of yore,_____
2. Strong - ly grasped each oth - er's hand, Sealed their friend - ship true,_____
3. Up through a - ges crowned with fame, Rose this he - ro clan,_____

Pledged they each an oath to keep Leal the love they bore.
Swore in life or death to stand By their cho - sen few.
Men of faith and no - ble aim, High - est type of man.

Phi - kei - a! Phi - kei - a! Rang their war - cry clear.

Eis - a - nar oud Eis - a - nar They sang and cher - ished dear.

Tell Me Why She Wears His Pin

Arr. Shelby Davis, Akron '51
Setting: Chester L. Alwes, Hanover '69

Phi Delta Theta
We'll always be True

Setting: Chester L. Alwes, Hanover '69

Phi Delta Theta For Aye

Walter Benjamin Palmer, Emory '77, Vanderbilt '80   Setting: Chester L. Alwes, Hanover '69

1. In eight - een hundr'd and for - ty - eight, Phi Del - ta The-ta for aye, The
2. But six at first we soon be-came, Phi Del - ta The-ta for aye, A
3. The peo - ple of this col - lege town, Phi Del - ta The-ta for aye, Have

1. year we Phis com - mem - o - rate, Phi Del - ta The-ta for aye.
2. Gre - cian Clan of won - drous fame, Phi Del - ta The-ta for aye.
3. of - ten heard of our re-nown, Phi Del - ta The-ta for aye.

Phi Del - ta The - ta, Phi Del - ta The - ta,

Phi Del - ta The - ta, Phi Del - ta The-ta for aye.

4.
The Greeks who fight with Sword and Shield,
  Phi Delta Theta for aye,
To other Greeks will never yield,
  Phi Delta Theta for aye.

5.
The girls do much admire our pin,
  Phi Delta Theta for aye,
The hearts of some we hope to win,
  Phi Delta Theta for aye.

Phi Delta Theta
Serenade Song

Hans Grueninger

Melody: Gene Pennington, De Pauw '38
Setting: Chester L. Alwes, Hanover '69

We'll sing our way in-to your hearts with a Phi Delt ser-e-nade;

The night is o'er, the dawn is near, stars be-gin to fade; A

hap-py dream ca-ress-es you, Phi Del-ta's love is true; We will

sing our way in-to your heart, with a Phi Delt ser-e-nade.

Eternal Praise

Tune: Carmen Ohio
Setting: Chester L. Alwes, Hanover '69

Hugh M. Gray, Ohio Wesleyan '28

Come, broth-ers, let us raise a toast To the pin we love the most; To

sword and shield we'll loy - al be, In de - feat or vic - to - ry.

To her col - ors white and blue We will be for - ev - er true; To

Phi Del - ta we'll al - ways raise Voic - es of e - ter - nal praise.

Hail, Hail, Phi Delta Theta

The Good Ship Phi

Not too fast; sturdy

1. A stur - dy crew of Phis are we; Yo -ho, Yo -ho, Yo - ho,_____ The brav - est lads up -
2. Each year this crew goes sail - ing off; Yo - ho, Yo -ho, Yo - ho,_____ With brand new crew and
3. Oh, we're the tough - est crew of boys that ev - er reefed a sail;_____ We nev - er bat - ten
4. There's many a crew that sails a - bout up - on this Col - lege Sea;_____ There's Del - ta Tau, and

1. on the sea; Yo - ho, Yo -ho, Yo - ho,_____ For we can man - age steam and sail and ships of ev - 'ry
2. of - fic - ers; Yo - ho, Yo -ho, Yo - ho,_____ The pi - lot steers us on our way, and ne'er a shoal strikes
3. down a hatch no mat - ter what the gale._____ When - e'er the sea is rough, boys, and the waves are roll - ing
4. Sig - ma Chi, and Be - ta and D. K. E._____They're all good crews with skip - pers bold; their speed we can't de -

poco rit.

1. sort;_____ And out - ride fierc - est winds and waves, and safe - ly make our port._____
2. he;_____ For he knows his course and puts all his force to win right lust - i - ly._____
3. high, Like ev - 'ry true broth - er we stick to each oth - er, this crew of the good ship Phi._____
4. ny; But have to hump to get the jump on the crew of the good ship Phi._____

Come Let Us Quaff A Stein

Words and Music by Rea Hanna, California 1900
Arranged by William Haid, Ohio State '24

XIII

Constitution & General Statutes

THE CONSTITUTION AND General Statutes which make up The Code of Phi Delta Theta are the laws of the Fraternity. These laws govern the structure of the Fraternity, the procedure of its various bodies, and the basic operation of the chapters. Although all chapters are autonomous and self-governing, they must obey the laws outlined in The Code. It is adherence to these basic laws that preserves the general similarity between each chapter of Phi Delta Theta.

The General Statutes are amended every two years at the General Convention. Proposals to change The Code are submitted to The Code Committee, a committee appointed by the General Council. Legislation is usually submitted in writing by any member of the Fraternity well in advance of the Convention, but changes are allowed to be submitted even during the Convention proceedings. Because each chapter has one vote, the majority of the votes at the Convention are in the hands of the undergraduate chapters' delegates. These chapter delegates propose legislation, debate motions, and vote for or against these amendments to the General

Statutes. On occasion, these debates become quite enthusiastic as the delegates try to make decisions that are best for the Fraternity.

The Constitution can only be amended by affirmative action at two consecutive General Conventions. The Constitution provides for the powers of the Convention and the General Council, indicates where alumni clubs and chapters may be established, and outlines some of the proper symbols and insignia of the Fraternity. It also gives requirements for membership.

After each Convention, two new copies of The Code are distributed to each chapter. These copies are usually kept by the president and secretary.

No chapter should have bylaws that conflict with any part of The Code. For this reason, it is important that each member understands The Code and how its laws apply to the chapter. Phikeias should read the copy of The Code found on the following pages.

THE CONSTITUTION
OF THE
PHI DELTA THETA FRATERNITY

PREAMBLE

We, who have accepted The Bond of the Phi Delta Theta Fraternity, recognizing it as a basis of union, and desiring to derive its benefits, do ordain and establish for the Phi Delta Theta Fraternity the following Constitution:

ARTICLE I—OBJECTS

1. *Relation to Bond.* The objects of this Fraternity are to instill, in all members, the high principles of The Bond of Phi Delta Theta and to attain an organized brotherhood that will assist all its members to conduct themselves at all times in accordance with these principles.

ARTICLE II—GENERAL CONVENTION

2. *Powers.* Subject to the provisions of this Constitution, supreme legislative and judicial powers are vested in the General Convention, composed of delegates from chapters and alumni clubs, of general officers of the Fraternity and such other officers as the General Statutes may designate.

3. *Statutes.* The General Convention shall enact Statutes for the government of the Fraternity, in accordance with this Constitution.

4. *Ritual.* The General Convention shall adopt a Ritual for the use of the Fraternity, which shall be in harmony with The Bond of the Phi Delta Theta.

5. *Next Convention.* The General Council shall determine the time and place of the next convention. Not more than three years shall intervene between such conventions, except, in the event of a state of war existing, the General Council may deem the holding of such convention inadvisable.

ARTICLE III—GENERAL COUNCIL

6. *Officers.* Each General Convention shall elect a General Council composed of a President and four additional members.

7. *Duties.* The General Council shall be the legal representative of the Fraternity and custodian of the property of the Fraternity. The General Council shall interpret and administer all laws of the Fraternity and make such policies and appointments as may be necessary to promote the general welfare of the Fraternity.

8. *Vote Required.* Every decision of the General Council shall require a four-fifths affirmative vote, except as provided in Section 9—Replacement of a Council Member.

9. *Replacement of Council Member.* Any member of the General Council may be removed from office for cause by the unanimous vote of the other four members. Any vacancy on the General Council, including the office of president, may be filled by a unanimous vote of the remaining members.

ARTICLE IV—CHAPTERS

10. *Where Located.* Chapters of the Fraternity shall be established and maintained only at accredited colleges and universities.

ARTICLE V—ALUMNI CLUBS

11. *Where Established.* Alumni club charters may be granted by the General Council upon petition of alumni residing in a particular locality.

ARTICLE VI—MEMBERSHIP

12. *Qualifications.* Each chapter shall select its members from among the male students who are in regular attendance at the college or university at which it is established, except in special cases as approved by the General Council.

Those chosen by the chapter must be men who exemplify friendship, sound learning and rectitude. (1996)

13. *Voting.* A person pledged to this Fraternity shall be chosen by the active members of the chapter in which he is proposed for membership, in accordance with the bylaws of that chapter.

14. *Obligation.* Every person, on being admitted to membership, shall accept The Bond of Phi Delta Theta, and the Constitution and laws thereon based, shall not cheat, wrong, or defraud a brother Phi, a chapter of Phi Delta Theta or the Fraternity in general, and shall never unite with a similar fraternity.

ARTICLE VII—INSIGNIA

15. *Badge.* The badge of the Fraternity is made of gold or platinum, and consists of a shield, with a scroll bearing the letters of Phi Delta Theta over the fesse and nombril points, an eye over the honor point, and a sword attached by a chain from the sinister chief point to the hilt. The sword shall always be worn with the shield, and both may be made of one piece, the sword appearing to pass diagonally back of the shield from the sinister chief point to the dexter base point. On the reverse the initials, the Bond number of the owner, and the title of his chapter shall be inscribed. The badge may be jeweled, and the scroll may be enameled in white and the eye in black.

16. *Colors.* The colors of the Fraternity are blue and white, or azure and argent.

17. *Open Motto.* The open motto of the Fraternity is: Ειζ ανηρ ουδειζ ανηρ.

18. *Coat-of-Arms.* The coat-of-arms of the Fraternity is emblazoned as follows: * Escutcheon: Azure, on a bend argent, between six mullets of the second, a sword proper point downward. Helmet: Proper, affrontee, visor closed, mantling of the first and second. Crest: A dexter arm embowed vambraced hurling a javelin all proper. Motto: Ειζ ανηρ ουδειζ ανηρ.

19. *Seal.* The great seal of the Fraternity consists of the escutcheon of the coat-of-arms, with the legend: "Great Seal of Phi Delta Theta Fraternity," and the figures "1848" in a circle about the same.

20. *Patron Goddess.* Pallas, Goddess of Wisdom, is recognized as the Patron Goddess of Phi Delta Theta.

21. *Secret Work.* The Fraternity's secret motto, grip, raps, passwords, test words and signs of recognition shall be transmitted orally and in no case may be reduced to print or writing except as the General Council shall provide. At each General Convention the General Council shall designate some member of the Fraternity who shall exemplify the unwritten work of the Fraternity.

---

* When depicted in colors the field is blue, the stars silver, the sword, helmet, mail on the arm and javelin gold, the hand flesh color, the mantling blue and silver, the wreath blue and silver, the motto of black letters on a white scroll.

ARTICLE VIII—COMMUNICATIONS *

22. *Communications.* The General Council shall determine what communication vehicles are to be developed by the Fraternity and provide for the production and distribution thereof. (2002)

ARTICLE IX—AMENDMENTS

23. *Amendment of Constitution and Ritual.* This Constitution and the Ritual of the Fraternity may be amended only by a three-fourths vote of any two successive General Conventions.

24. *Amendment of General Statutes.* The General Statutes may be amended only by a three-fourths vote of any General Convention.

25. *Proposed Amendments.* Proposed amendments to the Constitution, Ritual and General Statutes must be presented to the Convention in writing or print.

26. *Time of Vote.* A vote on proposed amendments to the Constitution and Ritual of the Fraternity can be taken no sooner than a session of the Convention on the day following their introduction. A vote on proposed amendments to the General Statutes may be taken on the day of their introduction.

---

* The 2000 & 2002 Convention revised ARTICLE VIII—PUBLICATIONS, giving it the new title as listed and making modifications to broaden the language given the increased use of technology in communications.

THE GENERAL STATUTES
OF THE
PHI DELTA THETA FRATERNITY

Laws of general application enacted by the General Convention based on, and subordinate to, the Constitution of the Phi Delta Theta Fraternity.

TITLE I—GENERAL CONVENTION

27. *How Composed.* The General Convention shall consist of the following delegates: General Council members, one member of the Walter B. Palmer Foundation Incorporated Board of Trustees, one member of the Phi Delta Theta Educational Foundation, one member of the Canadian Scholarship Foundation, and one member of the Frank J. R. Mitchell Scroll Fund Board of Trustees, the Province Presidents, or in their absence, the assistant or acting Province Presidents, Past Presidents of the General Council, the members of the Survey Commission, the Scholarship Commissioner, the Housing Commissioner, the Executive Vice President, the Finance Commissioner, the Fraternity Chaplain, the Fraternity Warden, and any other such commissioners as appointed by the General Council and Official Delegates of chapters and alumni clubs. (1998)

28. *Votes of Delegates.* Each delegate shall have one vote, but a delegate holding more than one office shall have only one vote. Voting by proxy is prohibited.

29. *Privileges of Visitors.* Members of the Fraternity not delegates to the convention shall be admitted thereto and may speak but may not vote or offer motions.

30. *Election of Delegates.* Every chapter in the Fraternity shall send an official delegate to each General Convention. At a regular meeting of the chapter in the university or college term immediately preceding the Convention, each chapter shall elect from its active members who will be in attendance during the following term, a delegate and an alternate. The chapter vice president shall immediately

forward to the General Headquarters of the Fraternity the names and classes of the delegate and alternate elect; and shall send like notice of any subsequent change.

31. *Credentials.* Delegates from chapters and alumni clubs shall present credentials. No delegate shall be seated from a chapter which is delinquent in money payments or required reports, except by majority vote of the convention.

32. *Rules of Order.* The General Convention shall be governed by parliamentary rules defined in *Robert's Rules of Order,* except where they conflict with the Constitution or statutes of the Fraternity, or the rules of order adopted by the convention.

33. *Quorum.* A quorum of the General Convention shall consist of a majority of the delegates present and entitled to vote.

34. *Ayes and Nays.* On a motion to grant or withdraw a charter all votes must be recorded by written ballot. On any vote to amend the Constitution, General Statutes, or Ritual, the ayes and nays shall be recorded. On demand of twenty-five of those entitled to vote, the ayes and nays shall be recorded on any question before the Convention.

35. *Officers.* The President of the General Council and the Executive Vice President of the Fraternity shall be *ex officio* the Chairman and the Secretary of the General Convention. The President shall appoint wardens who shall have charge of the approaches of the convention and shall admit no person not entitled to enter. (1972)

36. *Committees.* The General Council shall appoint such Convention committees as it may deem necessary.

37. *Resolutions and Motions.* The chairman of the General Convention may require any resolution or motion to be in writing.

38. *Effective Date of Legislation.* Unless otherwise specified, every enactment of the convention shall take effect upon the adjournment of the General Convention at which enacted.

39. *Printing and Distribution of Proceedings.* The General Council shall arrange for the printing and distribution of the "Journal of Proceedings" of the General Convention. The original manuscript of the "Journal" and reports shall be preserved.

TITLE II—GENERAL COUNCIL

40. *Appointment of Nominating Committee.* The General Council shall appoint a Nominating Committee of not less than seven members, at least one of whom shall be a Past President of the General Council and one of whom shall be an undergraduate delegate to the Convention. This committee shall be appointed at the first meeting of the General Council in the academic year following the Convention except that the undergraduate member shall be appointed before the Convention. The committee shall make recommendations on the nominees for the General Council. Each Province President shall be an advisory member of the committee, as well as any member in good standing in Phi Delta Theta.

The list of nominees for the presidency of the General Council and membership on the General Council shall be posted in a conspicuous place in the General Convention hall before the first general session of the General Convention.

A name or names may be added to these lists on the written application of at least twenty-five delegates, who are entitled to vote, presented to the Convention within twenty-four hours of the opening of the first general session of the General Convention. (1994)

41. *Election of President.* The Convention shall, by written ballot, first elect a President from the

final list of nominees for President. If upon the first ballot any one person shall receive a vote of over 50 percent of the total vote cast, such person without further ballot shall have been elected President. If, however, on such first ballot no person shall have received a vote of over 50 percent of the vote cast, the two persons receiving the highest number of votes shall be considered the nominees and another ballot taken and the one of these two nominees receiving the higher vote shall be elected the President.

42. *Election of Other Council Members.* The Convention shall then elect, by written ballot, four additional members to the General Council from the final list of nominees for the General Council which shall include any unsuccessful candidates for President.

Upon the first ballot, if more than four persons receive in excess of 50 percent of the total vote cast, the four persons receiving the highest number of votes shall be thereupon elected to membership to the General Council. In the event four persons are not so elected, the Convention shall continue, after dropping the nominee with the least number of votes each time, to ballot on the remaining nominees until all places on the General Council have been filled, it being necessary to obtain more than 50 percent of the total vote cast to be elected to this office. (1984)

43. *Term of Office.* The term of office of the President and members of the General Council shall be until their successors have been duly elected and installed.

44. *Installation of General Council.* The General Council elect shall be installed not later than the last session of the General Convention.

45. *Duties of President.* The President shall be responsible for directing the affairs of the Fraternity during his term of office and shall preside at all meetings of the General Council.

46. *Organization of the General Council.* The General Council shall elect one of its members to serve as Treasurer, one as Reporter, and two as Members-at-Large. The Treasurer shall supervise the finances of the Fraternity. The Reporter shall supervise the publications of the Fraternity. The Members-at-Large of the General Council shall perform such duties as may be assigned to them individually by the General Council.

The General Council shall appoint trustees of the Phi Delta Theta Educational Foundation and such other foundations and trusts which may from time to time be created.

The Frank J. R. Mitchell Scroll Endowment Fund, the Phi Delta Theta Educational Foundation and any similar funds or foundations heretofore created and maintained by the General Convention or the General Council shall continue in existence and be maintained and administered in accordance with the provisions of the General Statutes and any other relevant documents in existence and effective on August 25, 1970. In addition, the General Council shall have the power and authority to alter or amend any such provision, create additional provisions regarding the creation or administration thereof and to terminate and direct the distribution of assets of any such fund or foundation provided such distribution of assets would not conflict with the provisions of any other relevant documents pertaining to such fund or foundation. (1992)

47. *Eligibility for Re-election.* The President of the General Council shall be ineligible for re-election as President or as member of the General Council for the term next succeeding the term for which he was elected as President.

TITLE III—GENERAL HEADQUARTERS

48. *Establishment.* The Fraternity shall maintain a General Headquarters at the birthplace of the Fraternity, Oxford, Ohio.

49. *Executive Vice President.* The General Council shall employ an Executive Vice President who shall be in charge of the General Headquarters and who shall discharge the following duties:
(a) To act as Secretary to the General Council.
(b) To prepare and distribute supplies among the chapters and officers of the Fraternity.
(c) To collect all monies due the General Fraternity.
(d) To keep all accounts of receipts and disbursements.
(e) To visit active chapters and alumni clubs.
(f) To act as business manager of Fraternity publications.
(g) To employ sufficient clerical help to carry on the work of the Fraternity.
(h) To serve as a member *ex offcio* of the Survey Commission.
(i) Such other duties as the General Council may direct. (1990)

50. *Assistants.* The General Council may employ a member or members of the Fraternity to assist the Executive Vice President. (1990)

51. *Retirement.* The General Council shall establish terms and conditions for the retirement of qualified employees of the Fraternity.

TITLE IV—PROVINCES

52. *Division and Names.* The General Council shall divide the chapters into as many provinces as may be desirable for administrative purposes.

53. *Appointment and Qualifications of Province Presidents.* The General Council shall appoint a president for each province who shall serve for a two year term or until his successor is appointed. The General Council, through the General Headquarters, shall request the chapters within the province for a vote approving this appointment. If a majority of chapters vote against this appointment, the General Council shall withdraw such appointment and submit another appointment. The General Council may appoint assistants to any Province President. (1992)

54. *Duties of Presidents.* The president of each province shall have special charge of the interest of the Fraternity therein, and it is his duty to encourage and aid all chapters therein and promptly notify the General Headquarters of any matters which may require the attention thereof. The Province President or his assistant shall:
(a) Visit each chapter during the academic year in accordance with guidelines established by the General Council with regard to such visits.
(b) Make an official report after each chapter visit to the General Council.
(c) Give close supervision especially to the finances and scholarship of each chapter.
(d) Receive and check the monthly financial reports for each chapter.
(e) Aid the chapter in the collection of all dues, assessments, board and room accounts, house notes, etc., from active and alumni members, and make a report of all delinquents to the General Council with recommendations.
(f) Visit and cooperate with alumni clubs and help organize new ones.
(g) Arrange province meetings.
(h) In conference with the various chapters appoint Chapter Advisory Board Chairman making a report of these appointments immediately to General Headquarters. (1998)
(i) Prepare and distribute copies of the province meeting minutes to the following: (a) each chapter in the province; (b) each Chapter Advisory Board Chairman; (c) General Headquarters. (1998)

(j) Act as adviser to the Survey Commission concerning colleges or universities located within the bounds of his province.

(k) Consider complaints and make recommendations to the General Council with respect to financial delinquencies of alumni.

(l) The Province President or his assistant shall, in any case where he deems it desirable for the best interests of any chapter in his province, appoint a committee of alumni to consider any specific matter which he may wish to refer to said committee. Having investigated and considered the facts of the case, the committee shall inform the Province President of its findings and decision. If he approves of same, the Province President shall then immediately transmit the decision to the chapter concerned. In the event that any chapter shall fail to comply with such decision, the Province President shall forward a transcript of the case to the General Council with such recommendation as he may deem appropriate under the circumstances.

(m) Such other things as the General Council may order or request.

(n) Communicate and cooperate with the officers of the House Corporations within the bounds of his province, regarding Fraternity housing. (1994)

55. *Province Meetings.* The president of a province may call a province meeting at such a time and place as may be agreed upon. The expenses of holding a province meeting shall be borne by the chapters in the province.

TITLE V—ESTABLISHMENT, INSTALLATION AND WITHDRAWAL OF CHAPTERS

56. *Appointment of Survey Commission.* The General Council shall appoint a Survey Commission composed of not less than three members, at least one of whom shall be a Past President of the General Council. This commission shall be appointed at the first meeting of the General Council in the academic year following the convention. This commission shall make recommendations on the establishment of Colonies and the granting and withdrawal of charters. The Executive Vice President or his representative shall be *ex officio* a member of this commission, and each Province President shall be an advisory member of the commission concerning colleges or universities located within the bounds of his province. (2002)

57. *Achieving Chapter Status.* A group formed at an approved institution must first serve a period of time as a colony prior to a charter being granted. (1990)

58. *Establishing of a Colony.* An institution shall be approved for the establishment of a colony by the unanimous vote of the Survey Commission, the approval by the President in whose province the institution is located, and the unanimous vote of the General Council. Thereafter, the General Council may declare that either an existing group at the institution be granted colony status, or may direct the Survey Commission to form a colony at the institution so approved. (1990)

59. *Granting of Charters.* The Province President and the Survey Commission shall monitor the progress made by a colony. Upon successful completion of all General Council prerequisites, the Province President may recommend that a charter be granted. The recommendation must be approved by:

(a) Three-fourths of all chapters in the province in which the institution is located. Where there are three chapters, two thirds will be required.

(b) The Survey Commission.

(c) The General Council.

After all approvals have been given, a charter shall be granted. (1990)

60. (1990)

61. *Date and Names on Charter.* A charter shall bear the date on which the chapter was installed, and shall be signed by the General Council then in office. Chapters shall be entitled by the names of the states and Greek letters in alphabetical order according to the date of the establishment.

62. *Installation of Chapter.* A charter having been granted, the chapter shall be installed under the supervision of the General Council. The applicants having been initiated, the charter and copies of The Bond, Constitution, General Statutes, Ritual and other necessary books and papers shall be placed in their keeping, and they shall receive all needed instructions for organizing and conducting a chapter.

63. *Charter Revocation.* A petition for the revocation of a charter shall be referred by the General Council to the Survey Commission. The Commission shall make full investigation and report thereon to the next General Convention, which shall then have power to revoke the charter for cause. Such revocation shall require the affirmative vote of three-fourths of the General Convention.

64. *Charter Suspension.* The General Council, after full investigation and for just cause, shall have power to withdraw from a chapter the right to exercise all or any of its functions, except representation in the next General Convention. Such suspension shall not extend beyond the next General Convention. Representation of the suspended chapter at the General Convention shall include the right of members of the suspended chapter to be admitted to the General Convention and to speak, but no representative of the suspended chapter may vote or offer motions. (1982)

65. *Title Permanent.* In case of the revocation of a chapter for any cause, it shall not lose its title or chronological order in the records of the Fraternity.

66. *Charter Withdrawn.* When a charter is revoked or suspended, such charter shall be delivered to a person named by the General Council, together with all archives, books, membership records, and paraphernalia.

TITLE VI—ALUMNI CLUBS

67. *Name.* Alumni clubs shall be named after their localities.

68. *How Established.* A petition for the establishment of an alumni club at any place having been signed by not less than ten members of the Fraternity, shall be granted by the General Council.

69. *Alumni Club Membership.* Each Alumni Club may make reasonable regulations regarding admission of its members. No Alumni Club may suspend or expel a member from the fraternity, but where it learns that a member of the Fraternity is under suspension or is in financial arrears with his chapter or the General Fraternity, it shall not only refuse to admit such member to its membership, but shall refuse to retain such member in its membership. For failure to pay dues assessed by the club for its own support or other sufficient cause, the name of a member may be dropped from the roll of an Alumni Club.

70. *Officers.* Each alumni club shall have a president, vice president, treasurer, and such other officers as it may desire, said officers to be elected annually.

71. *Alumni Club Dues to General Fraternity.* During the fiscal year beginning July 1, each alumni club shall pay to the General Fraternity annual dues of twenty-five dollars ($25.00). (1992)

72. *Club Dues.* Every alumni club shall have the power to impose dues on its members for its own support.

73. *Meetings.* Every alumni club shall meet as often as it may decide but at least three meetings shall be held annually, one each in the fall, winter, and spring quarters. Founders Day shall be observed on or about the fifteenth day of March by each club, either individually or with other clubs.

74. *Letters to THE SCROLL.* The vice president of every alumni club shall promptly forward to the editor of THE SCROLL an account of the club's observance of Founders Day, and of other notable meetings during the year to meet published deadline dates for various issues. He shall also send to the editor personal items about the members, notices of deaths, and suggestions for possible feature articles.

75. *Delegate to Convention.* Every officially recognized alumni club which has conducted regularly stated meetings during the college year next preceding a General Convention, and which has paid its annual dues for the preceding biennium, may elect a delegate to the General Convention who, on payment of the regular convention fees, shall be entitled to one vote.

76. *Qualifications of Delegate.* No alumnus shall represent any alumni club in a General Convention unless he is a member of the club and a resident of the locality wherein it is established, and no active chapter member shall represent any alumni club.

77. *Withdrawal.* The charter of any alumni club may be withdrawn or its rights suspended in like manner as in the case of active chapters.

TITLE VII—CHAPTER MEETINGS AND OPERATION

78. *Regular Meetings.* Each chapter shall hold regular meetings conducted according to the ritual at least once every week while college is in session. For sufficient reasons the president of the chapter may postpone any regular meeting to a time not exceeding two weeks from the last regular meeting; in which case, the warden, unless another member be appointed instead, shall notify all active members of the time fixed.

79. *Special Meetings.* The president shall call special meetings whenever he or three other members may deem it advisable, and the warden, unless another member be appointed instead, shall notify all active members of any special meeting. It shall be the duty of active members to attend all regular and special meetings.

80. *Meetings Secret.* Meetings of chapters shall be secret, but the Memorial Ceremony may be in open session.

81. *Quorum.* A quorum in any chapter shall consist of a majority of the active members who are entitled to vote. This shall be sufficient for the transaction of business other than that specifically provided for in chapter bylaws, or the Constitution and General Statutes Sections 13, 151 and TITLE XVI. (1982)

82. *Order of Proceedings.* The order of proceedings of chapter shall be as follows:
(a) Opening Ceremony.
(b) Calling the Roll.
(c) Reading and Adopting the Minutes.
(d) Initiation, Affiliation or Reception Ceremony.
(e) Literary Exercises.
(f) Proposals for Membership.
(g) Reports of Officers.
(h) Reading Correspondence.
(i) Election or Installation of Officers.

(j) Reports of Committees.

(k) General Business.

(l) Anniversary, Valedictory, Alumni Day or Memorial Day Ceremony.

(m) Calling the Roll.

(n) Closing Ceremony.

This order, except as to opening and closing ceremonies and roll calls, may be changed by a majority vote.

83. *Pro Tempore Officers.* At the opening of meetings vacancies among the officers shall be filled *pro tempore* by the President. In case of the permanent absence of any officer, the chapter shall choose his successor.

84. *Founders Day Meeting.* Each undergraduate chapter shall meet on or about the fifteenth day of March to celebrate Founders Day. When convenient a college chapter and alumni club shall meet together.

85. *Chapter Dues and Assessments.* Each chapter shall fix its own initiation dues and affiliation dues, and have power to impose dues and assessments on its members for its own support. (1994)

86. *Guarantee Deposit Plan.* The General Council may require any chapter to operate under the Guarantee Deposit Fund plan.

TITLE VIII—CHAPTER EQUIPMENT

87. *Fraternity Supplies.* The supplies of the Fraternity, such as copies of the Constitution, General Statutes, Ritual, blank forms, etc., shall be distributed in such manner as the General Council may prescribe.

88. *Restrictions Concerning Bond.* On the establishment of each chapter, the Executive Vice President shall furnish it with a copy of The Bond, written in a durable book. Neither The Bond, nor any portion thereof, shall ever be written, type-written, printed, engraved or otherwise reproduced, except by a member of Phi Delta Theta, under the direction of the General Council. (1972)

89. *Distribution of Constitution and General Statutes.* The Constitution and General Statutes shall be printed and distributed in accordance with the directions of the General Council.

90. *Distribution of Rituals.* The Ritual of the Fraternity shall be printed and distributed in accordance with the directions of the General Council.

91. *Custody of Books.* During the collegiate year, the president of the chapter shall always keep The Bond and Rituals under secure lock and key, except when they are in use during meetings.

92. *Custody of Books and Records During Vacation.* At the last regular meeting in the collegiate year, each chapter shall determine what members shall have charge during vacation of The Bond and Ritual.

93. *Chapter Paraphernalia.* Each chapter shall provide itself with all the paraphernalia required by the Ritual.

94. *Approved Suppliers.* The General Council may select an approved supplier or suppliers who, in the manufacture of badges, Fraternity jewelry, stationery, paraphernalia and other Fraternity supplies, shall agree to conform to the designs or styles authorized and the standard of material and workmanship established by the General Convention or the General Council.

The General Council may suspend the approval of any such approved supplier or suppliers for making an unauthorized design or style, failing to maintain a creditable standard of material and workmanship, or in any manner failing to conform to the requirements established by the General

Convention or the General Council. The General Council may grant permission to any manufacturer or processor to use any of the Fraternity insignia or symbols in or upon jewelry, clothing, glassware, or article or commodity of any character or kind.

TITLE IX—CHAPTER HOUSES

95. *Chapter House Corporations.* No chapter shall become incorporated, but an association connected with a chapter but controlled by alumni of the Fraternity may be incorporated under applicable state, provincial or federal laws for the purpose of owning property for the benefit of the chapter, subject to the following considerations: (1) neither the name of the Fraternity nor the title given by the Fraternity to the chapter shall be used as the legal name of the corporation; (2) the chapter president and such other member of the active chapter as the said chapter may designate shall be voting members of the corporate board; and (3) the corporate charter and bylaws may contain provisions that in the event the charter of such local chapter is suspended or revoked, all assets will be preserved for the purposes of the chapter for a reasonable period of time and in a reasonable manner. Such provisions may, but need not necessarily or exclusively, contain provisions directing that in the event the charter of such local chapter is revoked, all assets of such corporation shall thereupon be transferred to the trustees of the Walter B. Palmer Foundation Incorporated. (1998)

96. *House Corporation Records.* The Trustees or officers of chapter house corporation shall keep appropriate records and books of account and an annual audit of same shall be furnished the active chapter and the General Council. (1996)

97. *Chapter House.* Every chapter shall have the right to rent either from its own chapter house corporation, or other lessor, a house for its members to live in.

98. *House Rules.* Every chapter occupying a chapter house must adopt strict rules for the government thereof, which are consistent with the Fraternity's risk management policies, and shall, among other things, prohibit all forms of vice in the chapter and which shall prohibit the use or presence of intoxicating liquors and all gambling in the chapter house where such use or presence is contrary to the rules and regulations of the college or university where the chapter is established. The use or presence of hallucinatory drugs or marijuana in any form is prohibited.

These house rules shall promote maintenance therein of a good moral atmosphere and provide for the preservation of good order and for the establishment of fixed and regular hours of study, adequate for the scholastic needs of its members. A printed or typewritten copy of the house rules shall be posted in the chapter house. (1992)

99. *House Occupancy.* During occupancy of the chapter house by the chapter as such, rooms may not be rented to anyone except members and Phikeias of the chapter who are enrolled as students in the college, except upon written permission of the Province President and Chapter Advisory Board Chairman. (1998)

100. *Pledged Men in Houses.* Pledged men may live in the chapter house for a period not to exceed one year preceding their initiation, provided that they be always carefully excluded from the ritualistic portion of the chapter meetings. (1976)

101. *Removal of Alumni or Phikeias.* The Province President shall have the authority to remove any alumnus or Phikeia from the house or property for cause, and such act of the Province President shall be final. (1992)

TITLE X—FINANCE

102. *Dues and Assessments.* The General Convention shall provide for the payment by active members at the time of their initiation of such initiation dues as may be necessary for the support of the Fraternity; but in case of emergency, a special per capita assessment may be levied upon them by the General Convention or by the General Council. (94)

102.1 *Dues Adjustments.* The General Council shall present to each General Convention a recommendation as to whether or not any adjustments should be made to initiation dues, Phikeia dues, annual membership dues, as well as the amounts to be collected for the Convention and Leadership Conference funds.

103. *General Fraternity Initiation Dues.* * (a) The chapter Treasurer shall forward to the General Fraternity the sum of sixty dollars ($60.00) with each Phikeia's biographical data card within ten days after Phikeia induction. (b) The chapter Treasurer shall forward to the General Fraternity the sum of two hundred twenty-five dollars ($225.00) for each initiate within ten days after initiation. (2004)

103.1 *Annual Membership Dues.* Each chapter of Phi Delta Theta shall pay to the General Fraternity the sum of seventy-five dollars ($75.00) per active member, per year. (2004)

104. *Allocation of Payment.* Of the said sum paid for each initiate, the General Council shall provide the initiate with a life subscription to *The Scroll* and *Palladium*, and shall in its discretion allot portions thereof to the following funds: The Walter B. Palmer Foundation Incorporated Fund, the Contingency Fund, or the General Fund. (1998)

105. *Voluntary Contributions.* The General Council shall solicit voluntary contributions from each alumnus member of the Fraternity. These contributions shall be distributed into the different funds of the Fraternity at the discretion of the General Council. (1980)

106. *Officers' Expenses to General Convention.* Each member of the General Council, each Province President, Past Presidents of the General Council, and any other General Officers so designated by the General Council shall be reimbursed for convention expenses. (1988)

107. *Delegates' Expenses to Convention.* Each chapter shall pay to the General Fraternity a sum not to exceed two hundred and fifty dollars ($250.00) as deemed necessary by the General Council, on April 15 and October 15 of each year, to be placed in a special fund and applied solely toward defraying the expenses of the active chapter delegates to, at, and from the meetings of the General Convention. Prior to each convention, the General Council shall determine the basis on which expenses of the delegates from chapters not delinquent in money payments to the General Fraternity shall be paid. Due notice of such delinquency shall be given by General Headquarters. (1998)

108. *Delegates' Expenses to Leadership Conference.* Each chapter shall pay to the General Fraternity a sum not to exceed one hundred dollars ($100.00) on April 15 and October 15 of each year to be placed in a special fund and applied solely toward defraying the expenses of the active chapter delegates, chapter advisory board chairmen, and other officers of the Fraternity to, at, and from the meetings of the Leadership Conferences. Each chapter in the Fraternity shall send an official delegation to a Leadership Conference. (1998)

109. *Meeting Attendance Required.* In the event that a delegate from an active chapter to a General Convention or Leadership Conference fails to remain in constant attendance at its sessions, or withdraws from the meeting before the final session thereof without first having obtained the consent of the General Council, the amount provided for his expenses shall be declared void and if a portion has been advanced to him, that portion shall become an obligation to the General Fraternity on the part of the delegate's chapter. If the amount so assessed is not paid by the chapter within six months

* *Effective July 1, 2005. This revised version of 103 was approved by the 2004 General Convention. Until the effective date, "Phikeia dues" will remain at $50.00 and "Initiation" dues will remain at $185.00.*

from the date of the convention, the Executive Vice President shall so report to the General Council for such action as may be deemed advisable. (1972)

110. *Officers' Expenses.* The members of the General Council and other General Officers shall be reimbursed for necessary expenses incurred in the discharge of their official duties.

111. *Salaries of Employees.* The General Council shall determine the compensation to be given to employees of the Fraternity.

112. *Official Audit.* All financial accounts of the General Fraternity shall be audited annually by certified public accountants employed by the General Council, and reports thereof shall be made to the General Council and to the succeeding General Convention. Special funds must be audited at least biennially.

TITLE XI—OFFICERS OF CHAPTERS

113. *Officers.* The officers of each chapter shall be a President, Vice President, Alumni Secretary, Secretary, Treasurer, Warden, Phikeia Educator, Recruitment Chairman, Historian, Chaplain, Chorister, Librarian, Awards Chairman, Scholarship Chairman, Foundation Representative, and Risk Management Chairman. (2002)

113.1 *Eligibility for Office.* Officers from each chapter shall be elected from the active members thereof. Members with scholastic delinquencies as stipulated in Section 149 of the General Statutes or members who are financially delinquent shall not be eligible for election to office or continuance in office. (1984)

114. *Terms of Office.* The Treasurer, Vice President, Historian, and Alumni Secretary shall be elected for one year and the other officers may be elected for each term in the year. (1972)

114.1 *Election Procedures.* The elections shall be at regular chapter meetings. Officers, convention delegates or other chapter representatives shall be elected by majority vote, by written ballot, except where there is but one nomination. Voting shall be under the direction of two tellers appointed by the President, one of them being the Warden, unless for personal reasons, he should be excused. (1972)

115. *Installation.* Officers shall be installed at the regular meeting next after their election, and they shall hold office until their successors are installed, when each shall surrender to his successor all the books, records, receipts and other property of the chapter in his possession. By a two-thirds vote of those present, officers may be installed before adjournment of the meeting at which they are elected.

116. *President.* The President of a chapter shall preside at all meetings thereof, and, within the chapter, shall enforce the laws and rules of the Fraternity. He shall be charged with the custody of The Bond, Constitution, General Statutes, Rituals, and Bylaws, and shall deliver them to his successor.

117. *Vice President.* The Vice President shall, in the temporary absence of the President, assume the full responsibilities of the President; serve as chairman of the Executive Committee and coordinate the activities of all the officers. He will be responsible for the preparation of all special reports as assigned by the President and shall supervise the Secretary in the preparation of all the routine correspondence and reports. (1996)

117.1 *Risk Management Chairman.* The Risk Management Chairman shall make the chapter aware of the risk management policies of the General Fraternity, the house corporation, and the university/college, and frequently report his activities to the President. (1996)

118. *Alumni Secretary.* The Alumni Secretary shall keep such a record of the alumni members of the chapter as shall be specified by the General Council, and shall transmit copies of all changes in data to the General Headquarters of the Fraternity. He shall endeavor to maintain close and cordial

relations between the chapter and its alumni by correspondence, and supervision of chapter publications.

119. *Secretary.* The Secretary shall prepare a permanent record of the proceedings of every meeting and shall record each roll call therein, one copy to be placed in the President's file and one to be maintained by the chapter.

The Secretary shall conduct the official correspondence of the chapter; give an account thereof at each meeting; preserve all official communications, and write newsletters for *The Scroll.*

120. *Treasurer.* The Treasurer shall collect all monies due the General Fraternity and the chapter, giving receipts therefor, and shall disburse the same according to generally accepted accounting procedures. He shall make all payments to the General Fraternity, and shall keep proper account books as prescribed by the General Council. He shall render a statement of the financial condition of the chapter monthly to the General Headquarters of the Fraternity, to the Province President and to his own chapter.

The books of the Treasurer, or other person having charge of the financial affairs of each chapter, shall have an audit, compilation, or review annually by a certified public accountant, or other qualified accountant, who is approved by the Province President and Treasurer of the General Council. Such audit, compilation or review shall be made at the conclusion of the chapter's fiscal year. Notice of the audit, compilation or review shall be made not later than June 30. The certified report, compilation or review of said auditors shall be prepared in triplicate. A copy shall be filed with General Headquarters and the Province President not later than September 30 and the remaining copy shall be retained by the chapter and be available at all times.

Upon failure to comply with these provisions, the Province President shall engage a certified public accountant or other qualified accountant to make the required audit and transmit certified copy of the report to General Headquarters. In such event, the expense of employing such auditors shall be paid by the General Fraternity and by it charged to the chapter whose books are so audited and shall be collected by the General Fraternity from the chapter in the same manner as other monies owing the General Fraternity. The Treasurer shall be bonded in the sum of at least $1,000, such bond to be procured in blanket form for all chapters by the General Headquarters of the Fraternity, the pro-rata cost to be borne by each chapter. (1984)

121. *Warden.* The Warden shall serve official notices, attend to the keeping of the chapter rooms, ensure that all required ritual paraphernalia is in proper order, and be responsible for the care of all chapter room equipment. He shall oversee and assist with all ritual activity of the chapter and he shall ensure The Bond is read and ritual ceremonies reviewed during a regular chapter meeting once each month. (1992)

121.1 *Phikeia Educator.* The Phikeia Educator shall be responsible for the supervision of Phikeia group activities, including their meetings and learning program. He shall uphold the laws and rules of the Fraternity regarding Phikeia education. (2002)

121.2 *Recruitment Chairman.* The Recruitment Chairman shall be responsible for developing and facilitating a year-round program for educating the chapter membership on methods of effective recruitment. He shall chair the chapter's Recruitment Committee and shall uphold the laws of rules of the Fraternity regarding enlistment of new members. (2002)

122. *Historian.* The Historian shall write a history of the chapter for the collegiate year that he holds office. At some meeting within the first four weeks of the following year, the history shall be read and, on approval by the chapter, transcribed in a durable book.

A complete personal and biographical record, pertaining to each Phikeia, and prepared on such standard form as may be prescribed by the General Council, shall be forwarded to General Headquarters within ten (10) days after formal pledging. This record is to be supplemented during the membership of the individual with such additional data as shall be furnished by the chapter at the time of his initiation, graduation and other significant events.

Within ten days of initiation, the historian shall forward to the General Headquarters, without delay, the names and Bond numbers together with the date of initiation of all new initiates on the standard form prepared for that purpose. (1998)

123. *Chaplain.* The Chaplain shall conduct the religious exercises of the chapter.

124. *Chorister.* It shall be the duty of the Chorister to improve the efficiency of the chapter in singing the songs of the Fraternity.

125. *Librarian.* It shall be the duty of the Librarian to develop and maintain a chapter library. Such library shall contain *The History of Phi Delta Theta, Catalogue of Phi Delta Theta, The Manual of Phi Delta Theta,* copies of *The Scroll, The Palladium,* and such other fraternity publications and literature that it may be possible to obtain.

125.1 *Awards Chairman.* The President shall appoint, or the chapter shall elect, an Awards Chairman. It shall be the responsibility of the Awards Chairman to make the chapter aware of awards granted by the General Fraternity, university, community, and chapter, and he shall be responsible for coordinating and forwarding the awards reports. (1980)

125.2 *Foundation Representative.* The President shall appoint, or the chapter shall elect, a Foundation Representative. It shall be the responsibility of the Foundation Representative to act as liaison between the Educational Foundation United States or the Scholarship Foundation Canada and the chapter. He shall be responsible for making the chapter members aware of the Foundation's support programs, including the availability of financial grants, as determined from year to year. He shall help coordinate the scholarship award nominations. (1990)

125.3 *Scholarship Chairman.* The Scholarship Chairman shall appoint such number of members he considers necessary to constitute a Scholarship Committee. It shall be the duty of this committee, with such assistance as it deems necessary, to promote the scholarship of the entire chapter. (1992)

126. *Chapter Officer Reports.* Each chapter shall through its proper officers make and forward promptly to the general officer requesting them, all reports, remittances, *The Scroll* letters, and answer all inquiries by return mail. Failure to do so within five days after receipt of request shall subject an offending chapter to such discipline as the General Council may determine, including such fines as the General Council may see fit to levy.

127. *Executive Committee.* Each chapter shall have an Executive Committee which shall consist of the President, Vice President, Treasurer and such other members as deemed necessary by the chapter. It is the duty of this committee to prepare an agenda for chapter meetings prior to such meetings and generally to direct the activities of the chapter.

127.1 *Risk Management Committee.* Each chapter shall have a Risk Management Committee which shall consist of the Risk Management Chairman, the Phikeia Educator, the member responsible for social activities of the chapter, the member responsible for management of the chapter facility, and the President. It is the duty of this committee to assist in the education of the chapter on risk management issues in all areas of operations. (1998)

127.2 *Recruitment Committee.* Each chapter shall have a committee composed of the Recruitment Chairman and at least three other members of the chapter whose duty is to organize and execute a sound recruitment program for the enlistment of new members. (2002)

128. *Finance Committee.* Each chapter shall have a Finance Committee which shall consist of the Treasurer, an executive officer of the Chapter House Association or interested alumnus, and such other members as deemed necessary by the chapter. The duty of the Finance Committee will be to prepare a budget covering all the necessary expenses of the chapter for the coming year, including all fixed charges on the chapter house property and such payments on the principal of the chapter house indebtedness as the terms of the obligation or obligations of such indebtedness may provide for, or in the absence of such definite terms, such payments as conservative financial policies may dictate. This budget must be approved by a majority vote of the chapter. In addition, the Finance Committee shall assist the Treasurer in the performance of his duties, particularly the collection of accounts receivable.

129. (1992)

130. *Vacancies Declared by Chapter or General Council.* By a two-thirds vote of those present a chapter may declare any of its offices vacant. For neglect of duty, the General Council, the Province President concurring, shall have power to declare any office in a chapter vacant. Such vacancies shall be promptly filled by election.

131. *Chapter Advisory Board Chairman.* The Province President shall select an adviser for each chapter in his Province from alumni members of the Fraternity nominated by the chapter. The term of office of the Chapter Advisory Board Chairman shall be the period between General Conventions. A Chapter Advisory Board Chairman may be removed by the General Council with the concurrence of the Province President. Interim appointments of the Chapter Advisory Board Chairman necessitated by any vacancies will be made by the Province President with the concurrence of the active chapter. A Chapter Advisory Board Chairman may appoint one or more assistants but he shall retain full advisory responsibilities. In the case of long and satisfactory service a chapter may confer upon an adviser the honorary title of emeritus but without further advisory obligations. (1998)

132. *Duties of Chapter Advisory Board Chairman.* It shall be the duty of the Chapter Advisory Board Chairman to visit the chapter frequently, to counsel with the chapter about its interests, to sign the copy of the monthly report of the chapter treasurer designed for the General Headquarters, and to act generally for the Fraternity in bringing important matters officially to the attention of the chapter. He shall also be invited to the Province Meetings. (1998)

TITLE XII—ELIGIBILITY FOR PLEDGING

133. *Proposals for Pledging.* When any person is proposed to a chapter for membership, every active member of the chapter shall be required to investigate the qualifications of that person for membership in the Fraternity and his worthiness as a future member of the Fraternity. Every member of the chapter shall be entitled to give a full expression of opinion as to the qualifications and worthiness of the person proposed for membership. No person shall be pledged to or become a member of the chapter until the chapter is satisfied of the worthiness of the person and that he meets the requirements for membership in the Fraternity, and until the active members of the chapter at the time the vote is taken, vote in accordance with their chapter's bylaws to extend to that person a bid to become a member. After a vote to extend such a bid, it shall promptly be extended to that person by the president or other designated officer of the chapter and shall remain open for acceptance by him for a reasonable period of time as determined by the chapter. Until any such bid has been accepted by the person proposed, the bid may be withdrawn and nullified by a vote of the active chapter in accordance with the chapter bylaws at the time said vote is taken. If a bid to a person proposed for

membership is nullified and withdrawn by such a chapter vote, that person may not thereafter become a member of the Fraternity unless he thereafter again receives the membership vote of the chapter as stipulated by that chapter's bylaws, extending to him a bid for membership. (1972)

134. *Further Information.* If any member of a chapter requests further information about a person proposed for membership before voting on the question of extending a bid to that person, the taking of the vote may be delayed for a reasonable length of time and the chapter may require the Warden to obtain the information.

135. *Phikeia Education.* No chapter of Phi Delta Theta shall indulge in any physical abuse or undignified treatment of its Phikeias or members; any violation shall be punishable by the General Council. (1994)

136. (1972)

137. *Title of a Pledge.* A person who has been pledged to join the Fraternity shall be known as a Phikeia (pronounced Fi-ki-a).

TITLE XIII—ELIGIBILITY FOR MEMBERSHIP

138. *Time of Initiation.* No person shall be initiated unless eight weeks, or more if required by the institution at which the chapter is located, shall have expired from the date upon which he shall have pledged to join the Fraternity except that the General Council shall have the right in special cases to permit a shorter period of time.

138.1 *Depledging.* A person may be depledged at any time preceding initiation by a vote of all members of the chapter in accordance with its bylaws. (1972)

139. *Fraternity Examination.* No person shall be eligible for membership until he has successfully completed his Phikeia training and has passed an examination testing his knowledge of all aspects of the Fraternity and the chapter. Such examination shall be conducted by the Phikeia Educator or any other person or persons appointed by the chapter and shall be based on the questions and materials in the current Fraternity Phikeia manual and such other matter as may be appropriate. The Phikeia Educator or other such appropriate persons shall report the results of such examination to the chapter at the regular meeting following such examination. (1998)

139.1 *Completion of Pledgeship.* Upon receipt of the aforementioned report, the chapter shall determine whether the Phikeia has satisfied the requirements of the chapter with respect to term of residence, scholarship, finances and conduct during the period of pledgeship. The chapter shall determine whether the Phikeia has satisfied the above requirements by a vote of members of the chapter, in accordance with its bylaws. Upon completion of such a vote, a successful Phikeia may be initiated. (1994)

140. *When Initiated.* A preparatory student may be pledged to join this Fraternity, but shall not be initiated until he shall have entered an accredited college or university. A Phikeia who has failed to meet the necessary requirements for initiation within one year from date of pledging shall be automatically depledged and shall not be eligible for repledging until another full term has elapsed, at which time he must again receive the membership vote of the chapter in accordance with its own bylaws. (1994)

141. *Graduate and Professional Students.* A person pursuing a graduate or graduate professional course where a chapter is established may be initiated.

142. *Initiation of Petitioning Group Members.* The General Council may authorize the initiation into Phi Delta Theta of members of any petitioning group which has been granted a charter by this

Fraternity, provided that nothing herein shall be so construed as to confer on any such member the right to demand initiation into Phi Delta Theta.

143. *Membership in Other Societies.* When any person is considered for an invitation to unite with the Fraternity, he shall be required to name all secret societies of which he is or has at any time been a member or pledge.

144. *Double Fraternity Memberships Prohibited.* No person who is or has been a member of a general college fraternity similar to Phi Delta Theta shall be eligible to membership in Phi Delta Theta. A college organization of a strictly local character recognized by the college or university at which it was established is not construed to be a similar fraternity. However, no member of Phi Delta Theta may be a member of such a local organization as defined above at the same institution.

145. *Membership in Local Societies.* No member of Phi Delta Theta shall join any general or local society existing at the institution where his chapter is established, in case his chapter shall have adopted a By-Law or passed a vote forbidding its members to join such society; and should internal dissensions be caused by membership in such societies, the General Convention or the General Council shall have the power to prohibit members of Phi Delta Theta from joining such societies at particular institutions.

146. *Literary and Honorary Societies Excepted.* Nothing herein shall be construed to prevent a member of Phi Delta Theta from uniting with a strictly literary society, or an open and purely honorary fraternity.

TITLE XIV—RIGHTS AND OBLIGATIONS OF MEMBERSHIP

147. *Chapter Members.* Every person initiated shall be an active member of the initiating chapter so long as he shall pursue an undergraduate course of study at the institution where said chapter is established, unless he is expelled, suspended or is permitted to resign in accordance with the laws of the Fraternity. If an active member receives an undergraduate degree, or completes four full years of undergraduate study, or enters upon graduate study, graduate professional study, or any similar advanced course of study, he may elect to remain an active member, enjoying all privileges and obligations thereof, so long as he shall pursue said studies and comply with all the laws of the Fraternity.

148. *Rights and Obligations.* Every active member shall be required at all times to conduct himself in accordance with The Bond of Phi Delta Theta and the highest principles and traditions of the Fraternity. He shall be liable for all dues and assessments levied by his chapter. He is required to attend all meetings of his chapter and privileged to make motions, to vote and to hold office in his chapter subject to any section inconsistent herewith, except that no provision of this section or any other section of the Constitution and General Statutes shall be so construed as to forfeit the right of any member to vote on the question of membership, including pledging, depledging and separation from membership in the Fraternity. An alumnus member shall have the same right as an active member to attend meetings of his chapter and to speak on any motion.

149. *Scholarship.* Any active member of Phi Delta Theta, who, for one academic year, attains an average scholastic rating that is below the average scholastic rating required by the college or university for graduation, shall be deprived ipso facto of the privilege of voting in the chapter except on the question of membership, including pledging, depledging, and separation from membership in the Fraternity, until such time as his rating is above the rating required by the college or university for graduation.

150. *Name of Fraternity in Business Prohibited.* No member of Phi Delta Theta may use the name of the Fraternity or the name of any chapter in connection with any business enterprise.

TITLE XV—AFFILIATION

151. *Affiliation in Another Chapter.* Should a member withdraw from a college or university where he is a chapter member and enter another institution where there is a chapter, he may become formally affiliated with the latter chapter under the following conditions:

1. He has been in attendance in the latter institution at least one term.
2. His grade point average at the latter institution is equal to or above that required for initiation.
3. He has obtained from the former chapter and presented to the latter chapter an affiliation certificate which shall be granted by the former chapter if he is in good standing.
4. The chapter affiliating the member has voted to do so by a vote in accordance with the bylaws of the chapter. (1972)

152. *Where Affiliation Certificate Is Refused.* If, for any reason, a member should be refused affiliation in another chapter, he shall not be permitted to attend the meetings of that chapter or to live in its house or lodging. (1978)

*TITLE XVI—DISCIPLINE AND LOSS OF MEMBERSHIP (1982)

153. *Loss of Membership.* No member's connection with Phi Delta Theta may be severed except by expulsion as herein provided or by voluntary resignation made in writing by the member and accepted by a four-fifths (⁴/₅) vote of the General Council. (1982)

154. *Discipline by Chapter.* A chapter may discipline an active member of the chapter by:
(a) expulsion from membership;
(b) suspension from membership for a stated period of time not to exceed twelve (12) months;
(c) fine. (1982)

155. *Cause for Discipline.* An active member of the chapter may be disciplined by the chapter for any one or more of the following causes:
(a) financial delinquency;
(b) violation of The Bond, Constitution or General Statutes of the Fraternity;
(c) conduct unworthy of a member of Phi Delta Theta. (1982)

156. *Procedure for Discipline by the Chapter.* A chapter shall exercise its powers of discipline only after full investigation and for just cause. The active member sought to be disciplined shall be given notice in writing by the Warden of the alleged cause for his discipline and of the time and place at which a meeting of the chapter will be held to consider the matter. The notice in writing to the member sought to be disciplined shall be delivered no later than seven (7) days prior to the meeting of the chapter and shall be mailed to the member's last known address by registered mail, return receipt requested, or hand delivered by the Warden to the member sought to be disciplined. When said notice to the member sought to be disciplined is by registered mail, return receipt requested, delivery shall be deemed to have been made the date the notice is placed in the mail. The members of the chapter shall likewise be given notice by the Warden no later than seven (7) days prior to the meeting of the chapter by posting the notice in such a place where notices to members of the chapter are customarily posted. A meeting of the chapter shall then be held to decide upon such discipline and any vote to discipline the member shall only be effective if passed by a two-thirds (⅔) vote of members

---

* The **1982** Convention totally revised TITLE XVI—LOSS OF MEMBERSHIP, giving it the new title as listed and replacing Sections 153-173 with new Sections 153-164.

of the chapter who are present, provided that at least a majority of the active members who are entitled to vote are present. The President of the chapter shall promptly report any action of discipline in writing to General Headquarters.

Any member may initiate the procedure for discipline by a chapter by request made either verbally or in writing to the Executive Committee of that chapter.

The Executive Committee shall decide whether the matter should be brought before a meeting of the chapter. If the Executive Committee decides that the matter should not be brought before a meeting of the chapter, it shall report this decision and the reasons therefore to a meeting of the chapter. If the Executive Committee decides that the matter should be brought before a meeting of the chapter, it shall take all necessary action to do so and may, if it considers it advisable, appoint a special committee to investigate the matter and report to the meeting of the chapter held for the purpose of deciding upon any discipline. (1992)

157. *Reconsideration and Appeals.* A chapter may, by two-thirds (⅔) vote of members who are present, reconsider any decision imposing discipline on an active member or former member and reach the same or a different decision, provided that at least a majority of the active members who are entitled to vote are present. Any such action resulting in a different decision shall be promptly reported in writing to General Headquarters and to the Province President by the President of the chapter.

An active member, or former member, who has been disciplined by a chapter may appeal such decision to the General Council or the next succeeding General Convention if the decision has been sustained by the General Council. (1982)

158. *Discipline of an Alumnus Member by the General Council.* An alumnus member may be disciplined for any one or more of the causes set out in Section 155, by action of the General Council after full investigation and for just cause. A four-fifths (⅘) vote of General Council shall be necessary for such discipline. General Council may act to discipline an alumnus member upon the written request of an active chapter and with the approval of the Province President. (2000)

158.1 *Discipline of an Alumnus Member by the Chapter.* After seeking advice from and consulting with the Province President, a chapter may discipline an alumnus member of the chapter for any one or more causes set out in Section 155 by those means set out in the Section 154(a) or (b). The chapter shall act only after full investigation and for just cause.

The alumnus sought to be disciplined shall be given notice in writing of the alleged cause for his discipline and he shall be entitled to appear before or make written representations to the chapter. This notice in writing shall be delivered no later than ten (10) days prior to the date on which the action shall be taken by the chapter and shall be forwarded via registered mail, return receipt requested, to the member sought to be disciplined. Delivery shall be deemed to have been made the date the notice is placed in the mail. Any vote to discipline an alumnus shall only be effective if passed by a two-thirds (⅔) vote of members of the chapter who are present, provided that at least a majority of the active members who are entitled to vote are present.

The chapter shall forward a report of the disciplinary action taken to the Province President and the General Headquarters.

An alumnus member, or former member, who has been disciplined by a chapter may appeal such decision to the General Council or the next succeeding General Convention if the General Council has sustained the decision. (2000)

159. *Discipline by General Council.* An active or alumnus member may be disciplined by the

General Council in the manner set out in Section 154 and for the causes set out in Section 155. The General Council shall exercise its powers of discipline only after full investigation and for just cause. The member sought to be disciplined shall be given notice in writing of the alleged cause for his discipline and he shall be entitled to make written representations thereon to the General Council. The notice in writing shall be delivered no later than ten (10) days prior to the date on which action shall be taken by the General Council and shall be forwarded via registered mail, return receipt requested, to the member sought to be disciplined. When said notice to the member sought to be disciplined is by registered mail, return receipt requested, delivery shall be deemed to have been made the date the notice is placed in the mail. A four-fifths ($4/5$) vote of General Council shall be necessary for such discipline. (1992)

159.1 *Discipline by Province President.* After full investigation, a member may be disciplined by a Province President for the causes set out in Section 155. The Province President may suspend a member from membership for a stated period of time not to exceed twelve months and shall report his actions immediately to the General Council and the reasons therefore. He may recommend expulsion of a member to the General Council. Any appeal by an active or alumnus member, or former member, of a decision on discipline made by the Province President, shall be decided by the General Council only after full investigation and for just cause. (1986)

160 *Reconsideration by General Council and Appeals.* General Council may by a four-fifths ($4/5$) vote, reconsider any decision imposing discipline on an active or alumnus member, or former member, and reach the same or a different decision.

An active or alumnus, or former member, who has been disciplined by General Council may appeal such decision to the next succeeding General Convention. (1982)

161. *Procedure on Appeals to the General Convention.* Any appeal by an active or alumnus member, or former member, of a decision on discipline made by a chapter or the General Council shall be decided by the General Convention only after full investigation and for just cause. For this purpose, the General Convention may delegate to a committee the power to investigate and report. A two-thirds ($2/3$) vote of a quorum of the General Convention shall be necessary to decide any matter of discipline. (1982)

162. *Reconsideration by the General Convention.* The General Convention, by a two-thirds ($2/3$) vote of a quorum of the General Convention may reconsider any decision imposing discipline on an active or alumnus member, or former member, and reach the same or a different decision. Such reconsideration shall not take place except at the General Convention next succeeding that General Convention when the original decision was made. (1982)

163. *Effect of Expulsion from Membership.* A person expelled from membership in Phi Delta Theta shall forthwith surrender to the General Council, or its representative, his badge and all Fraternity property in his possession. Expulsion from membership terminates absolutely all rights, privileges and immunities of membership in Phi Delta Theta. (82)

164. *Effect of Suspension from Membership.* A person suspended from membership in Phi Delta Theta shall lose all rights, privileges and immunities of membership in Phi Delta Theta during the period of his suspension. He may not hold office, vote or attend chapter meetings. He may not reside in the chapter house without the written permission of the Province President and the Chapter Advisory Board Chairman. (1996)

165 - 173. (1982)

TITLE XVII—ALUMNI MEMBERS

174. *Alumni Members.* Any member who has withdrawn from the institution in which the chapter of his initiation is located or has been graduated therefrom shall be an alumnus member of the chapter of his initiation.

TITLE XVIII—INSIGNIA

175. *Use of Badge Design.* The manufacture of articles bearing the badge is prohibited, except as specially authorized by the General Convention. The General Council may authorize the manufacture and sale of such articles bearing the letters ΦΔΘ or a monogram of them, or the coat-of-arms of the Fraternity or other suitable emblematic design.

176. *Badge—How Worn.* Every member shall wear the badge at all appropriate times while he is attending college, the proper place for it being over the heart. The badge shall not be worn except by members of the Fraternity or their mothers, wives, daughters, sisters or fiancées. A penalty of up to one year's suspension from all rights and privileges of the Fraternity may be imposed on the member violating this latter section. (1980)

177. *Undue Display Prohibited.* Use of the crest, badge, or other symbols of the Fraternity in such a way as to bring discredit to the organization shall be prohibited.

178. *Fraternity Flag.* The Flag of the Fraternity consists of three perpendicular bars of equal width; the outer bars of blue and the inner bar of white material; each of the outer bars charged with three white five pointed stars; and the middle bar charged with the letters ΦΔΘ in blue; the stars and letters being arranged vertically; the hoist of the Flag on the staff being two-thirds of the fly; the staff having a spear-shaped head, the head, cord and tassels being silvered.

179. *Fraternity Banners.* The Fraternity banner has the form of an equilateral triangle and bears across the body the word "Miami" over the figures "1848"; above the left Φ; below Δ; and above the right Θ. The body is of blue material, the lettering in gold; the standard, if one is used, bar, cord and tassels being silvered. The banner for each chapter is similar except that for "Miami" and "1848" are substituted the name or initials of the institution at which the chapter is established and the year when the chapter was chartered.

180. *Phikeia Button.* The Phikeia button of the Fraternity is square, with slightly rounded corners, and is enameled in blue, with a bend enameled in white; on the bend, the letters "Phikeia" in gold; above the bend, three five pointed stars in gold, and as many below.

181. *Golden Legion Button.* The Golden Legion button shall be of such design as the General Council may approve. (1978)

181.1. *Silver Legion Button.* The Silver Legion button shall be of such design as the General Council may approve. (1992)

182. *Alumnus Charm.* The Alumnus Charm is of the same design as the pledge button, except, however, that the Greek letters of Phi Delta Theta replace the word "Phikeia."

183. *Recognition Button.* The recognition button is a small gold, silver or platinum button in the form of a coat-of-arms or the Greek letters ΦΔΘ.

184. *Badge of Mourning.* The badge of mourning consists of a black ribbon attached to the back of the Fraternity badge.

185. *Flower.* The flower of the Fraternity is the white carnation.

186. *Fraternity Whistle.* The whistle of the Fraternity is according to the following notation:

Index

Acknowledgments

Chapter Three, "History of Greek Societies," adapted from Baird's Manual of American College Fraternities, 20th Edition.
Chapter Five, "The Organization," written by M. Scott Mietchen, *Utah '84*.
Chapter Six, "The Chapter," written by Martin M. Taylor, *Marshall '89*, revisions by Nathan P. Thomas, *Southeast Missouri State '95*.
Chapter Seven, "Scholarship & Sound Learning," written by Dr. Edward G. Whipple, *Hanover '74*, and James C. Hoppe, *McMaster '87*.
Chapter Ten, "Risk Management," written by David C. Slatton, *Whitman '90*, and revisions by Marc S. Mores, *Iowa State '94*.

Photo Credits. Page 20 photo courtesy of the National Interfraternity Conference; page 32, photo copyright © the Colonial Williamsburg Foundation, Williamsburg, Va.; page 60, photo courtesy of Sean F. Keefer; page 79, photo copyright © 1992 by Hans Scott; page 80, photo courtesy of Sean F. Keefer; page 100, photo courtesy of Sean F. Keefer; page 109, photo of Lou Gehrig from United Press International; page 111, photo of Neil Armstrong copyright ©, National Aeronautics and Space Administration; thank you also to the many businesses, agencies, and organizations that submitted photos of "Famous Phis."

Thank you to Cynthia A. Phair for making all the updates and corrections to this edition. Thank you to Barbara Cotterman for assisting in organizing the revision process and thank you to Carmalieta Dellinger Jenkins for assisting in the proofing process.